COMMUNICATION: THE ART OF UNDERSTANDING AND BEING UNDERSTOOD

Communication:

THE ART OF UNDERSTANDING AND BEING UNDERSTOOD

a report on the
Seventh Communications Conference
of the Art Directors Club
of New York

ROBERT O. BACH, *Editor*

Communication Arts Books
Hastings House, Publishers
New York 22

this book designed by **ARTHUR HAWKINS**

Library of Congress Catalog Card Number: 63-13564
Published simultaneously in Canada by
S. J. Reginald Saunders Ltd., Publishers, Toronto 2B
Printed in the United States of America

CONTENTS

Foreword

This is the report of the seventh annual two-day Communications Conference in a stimulating series sponsored by the Art Directors Club of New York. It was attended by over 300 creative people — designers, artists, photographers, illustrators, film-makers, art directors, writers, educators, executives — each willing to expend time and energy to explore how better to *communicate* with one another, and with the audience he aims to reach.

The speakers and discussion leaders — all men of stature and international reputation in their respective areas of communication — opened eyes, ears and minds through their expressions of creative philosophies. The power of the written word (and of sound) in conjunction with pictures was reaffirmed. The universality of visual communciation regardless of language differences was forcefully demonstrated. The search for truth, beauty and reality was reiterated.

These Conferences are designed to excite, to inspire and, concurrently, to educate all concerned with the creative process. It is our intention to preserve as many as possible of the stimulating ideas which grew out of this meeting, and to make them available to a wider audience through this book.

Robert O. Bach, *Conference Director*

Arthur Hawkins, *Conference Chairman*

Biographical Notes on the Contributors

ROBERT O. BACH

A native San Franciscan, he studied at the California School of Fine Arts, followed by varied work as a designer and four years in the Air Force. Shortly after his return to civilian life, Mr. Bach joined N. W. Ayer & Son, Inc. and has since served as account representative and art director in their San Francisco and Honolulu offices before being recalled to the Philadelphia headquarters where he is now Vice President and Managing Art Director. A founding member and past president of the Art Directors Club of San Francisco, he was the first person from the West Coast to hold office in the National Society of Art Directors, and he is currently active in both the Philadelphia and New York Art Directors Clubs in addition to lecturing.

SAUL BASS

New York born, he has achieved an enviable international reputation as a designer concentrating, for more than 15 years primarily in motion pictures. Best known by the public for his titles to such films as "Around the World in 80 Days," "Anatomy of a Murder," "West Side Story," "Spartacus," and a host of others, Mr. Bass has also designed many award-winning advertising campaigns including those for "The Man With the Golden Arm," "Bonjour Tristesse," "Exodus." He has, in fact, won more than 50 national awards including that of the National Society of Art Directors' "Art Director of the Year (1957)."

KEN BAYNES

English by birth and education, Mr. Baynes was for several years Assistant Editor of the highly regarded international graphic arts magazine, *Graphis*, published in Zurich, Switzerland. A painter and an artist in stained glass, he also publishes his own magazine, *Number*, in London where he now lives and works.

AUSTIN BRIGGS

Always having had a way of "getting places," he started by being born in a railroad car while going through Humboldt, Minnesota. He is also restless in regard to his own work, having extended his talent to television, posters, portraits, book illustrations, and has even designed a stock certificate. One of our best known, most talented and hardest working illustrators, Mr. Briggs has experimented in all media with the sole idea of producing better pictures — including study and work in Paris for the entire year 1962. A winner of numerous gold medals and other awards in art directors and illustrators exhibitions, he is one of the original faculty of the Famous Artists Schools in Westport, Connecticut.

OLEG CASSINI

European born, he began his career in Florence sketching gowns for his mother's dress salon but has, paradoxically, devoted most of his life to promoting American fashion design. Moving on to Paris, then to Rome, to Hollywood and, subsequently to New York, Mr. Cassini numbers among his clientele many of America's most noted women including our First Lady, Mrs. Jacqueline Kennedy.

CHARLES T. COINER

A native Californian, he studied at the Chicago Academy of Fine Arts and still continues an active interest in art education. Mr. Coiner has been called a "triple-threat communicator" — art director, painter and educator. Now Vice President and Executive Art Director of N. W. Ayer & Son in Philadelphia, he pioneered the use of fine art for advertising and was named the first "Art Director of the Year" by the National Society of Art Directors when this award was initiated in 1949.

WILLIAM R. DUFFY

A pioneer in in television, he has created or developed many of the "firsts" that are now considered accepted procedures. He is best known, however, for his continuous efforts in behalf of the industry's creative growth as founder, and many times chairman, of award-giving groups and as author of scores of articles in the trade periodicals. Mr. Duffy is active in the National Academy of Television Arts and Sciences, the International Radio and Television Society, and as a teacher of creative television at New York University and Pratt Institute. As a Senior Art Director in charge of television at McCann-Erickson, Inc., New York, he is also consultant to all branch offices and affiliates throughout the world.

RALPH E. ECKERSTROM

Director of Design, Advertising and Public Relations of the Container Corporation of America, the scope of that title is a tribute to his talent and his dedication to good design. Yet he manages to find time to devote to important related activities, including service on the Boards of Governors of the American Institute of Graphic Arts and the Philadelphia Museum School of Art, the Visiting Committee for Carnegie Institute of Technology, instructor of industrial design at the University of Illinois, and as Chairman of the International Design Conference (1962) at Aspen, Colorado.

ARTHUR HAWKINS

A native of Maryland, a graduate of the University of Virginia, he received his art training at the Art Students League where he served as a member of the Board of Control. He has since been Eastern Art Director of Outdoor Advertising Incorporated, head art director for several medium-sized advertising agencies, a consulting art director and designer. He has edited four books on advertising art and designed several others. He is a past president of the Art Directors Club of New York and was charter secretary-treasurer of the National Society of Art Directors. The 1962 Visual Communications Conference was the second of which he served as chairman. He is a Sunday painter.

S. I. HAYAKAWA

Born in Vancouver, British Columbia, a graduate of the University of Manitoba and with advanced degrees from McGill University and the University of Wisconsin, Dr. Hayakawa is internationally known for his work in semantics. In addition to holding the chair of Professor of Language Arts at San Francisco State College, he edits the professional journal, *ETC.*, for the International Society of General Semantics. He is the author of many books, including the widely read *Language in Action* and *Language in Thought and Action.*

ART KANE

New York born and a graduate of Cooper Union School of Art, he turned from art direction of *Seventeen* magazine several years ago to devote full time to photography, in which he has won numerous gold medals and other top awards in exhibitions. A past instructor in design at Pratt Institute and the New School, Mr. Kane's work has appeared in such diverse publications as *McCall's, Look, Life, Horizon, Seventeen, Glamour* and *Sports Illustrated.* In advertising photography, his work has ranged from "travel" to "cosmetics," from "food" to "industrials," from "furniture" to "pharmaceuticals."

HENRY KOERNER

Coming from Vienna, he had his first showing of postwar Germany at New York's Midtown Galleries which immediately established him as one of our most interesting contemporary painters, and his works are now included in the collections of a number of leading museums. During World War II, Mr. Koerner was with the O.W.I. and O.S.S. in England and Germany, remaining in Berlin for two years with the Graphics Division of the Military Government. He has served for two years as artist in residence at Pennsylvania College for Women in Pittsburgh, where he now lives.

H. DONALD LA VINE

A pioneer in the increasingly important field of international commercial TV, he has written and supervised production of numerous commercials currently running in Latin America, Europe, Asia and Australia. Mr. LaVine is creative group head for international radio, television and cinema at McCann-Erickson, Inc.

SAMUEL MAGDOFF

Executive Producer of Elektra Film Productions, Inc., New York, he has many award-winning commercials at international film festivals to his credit.

GEORGE McNEIL

Born in New York City, he studied at Pratt Institute, the Art Students' League and the Hans Hofmann School of Fine Arts. Mr. McNeil has had nine one-man shows and a long list of important national exhibitions which have established him as one of the most advanced painters in the field of abstract art. A former instructor at the University of California he is currently Professor of Art History at Pratt Institute.

GEORGE NELSON

Born in Hartford, Connecticut, he graduated from Yale and studied at the American Academy in Rome. While Mr. Nelson concerns himself primarily with industrial design, as an architect and writer his interests and activities range far afield, including the design of the United States' exhibit in Moscow and the "Atoms for Peace" for the Atomic Energy Commission Exhibit in Cairo. He is the innovator of the storage-wall, the L-shaped desk, the bubble lamp and many other creations which we now all take for granted. He has taught at Yale and Columbia Universities and at Pratt Institute in addition to writing numerous books and magazine articles on architecture and design. He is the president of George Nelson, Inc.

ROBERT OSBORN

A mid-westerner, he studied at the Universities of Wisconsin and Yale then, in serious pursuit of art, at the British Academy in Rome and the Academie Scandinav in Paris. Mr. Osborn has been called "an individualist of great moral courage, an articulate spokesman as well as a marvelous draftsman, the eyes and ears of his generation as seen in the satires he has published over the years" including *Low and Inside*, *On Leisure* and *The Vulgarians*.

SILAS H. RHODES

Founder and, for more than 15 years, director of the School of Visual Arts in New York, Dr. Rhodes is a vigorous and creative educator. Having decided that outstanding artists should teach while at the *peak* of their careers rather than when they were on the decline, he has some 70 leading artists on his faculty today. With a view to broadening the humanities courses, he brought in distinguished poets, philosophers, writers, composers, dancers, architects. A member of the National Committee on Art Education and other educational groups, he is also the author of *New Concepts in the Teaching of Art*.

GILBERT SELDES

Devoting most of his professional life to work in, and criticism of, popular entertainment, he has been described as a "career non-comformist in the world of ideas." After a notable career in radio, he created the Television Program Department of CBS and helped to produce the historical feature film "This is America." His *The Seven Lively Arts* was published in 1924, followed by studies of new approaches to the mass media in *The Great Audience* and *The Public Arts*. His articles on mass communication, particularly television, have appeared regularly in the *Saturday Review* and *TV Guide*. Mr. Seldes is now Dean of the Annenberg School of Communications, University of Pennsylvania.

on understanding and being understood

DR. S. I. HAYAKAWA
Professor of Language Arts,
San Francisco State College

What are the conditions of success or failure in communication? Or, to put it another way, why do people welcome some communications and accept ideas or suggestions eagerly some of the time, and strenuously reject or studiously ignore other communications? And if our own communications are ignored or rejected, is there anything that can be done about it?

In order to discuss these questions, I am going to start by presenting a broad theory of human behavior in terms of which to try to understand the act of communication.

The fundamental motive of human behavior is not self-preservation, but preservation of the symbolic self.

What I call the symbolic self is pretty much the same thing as what Carl Rogers and others call the "self-concept," what Andras Angyal calls the "self-organization," and what still others call the "self-structure." *So let me state the law in the form given by Carl Rogers: first, that "the basic purpose of all activity is the protection, maintenance, and enhancement of the self-concept," and secondly, that "the self-concept or self-structure may be thought of as an organized configuration of perceptions of the self which are admissible to awareness."*

10 In other words, human beings are hopelessly addicted to the processes of abstraction and symbolization, which are the distinguishing features of their survival mechanism. Hence human beings, in addition to abstracting and symbolizing the data of their environment, abstract and symbolize about themselves. Each of us possesses not only a self, but also a self-concept — that the self-concept is not what you are, but what you think you are.

The self-concept: determinant of our behavior

The self-concept then is the sum-total of the things we feel we know about ourselves, including our past history, our present condition, status, and role, our ideals, our plans for the future, our estimates of our own relationships with others: "I am thin (or fat)," "I am a good mixer," "I pay my debts promptly," "I am poor at arithmetic," "I shall never be a millionaire," "I am beautiful," "Nobody loves me," "I have less money than Bill, but more brains," "I have less brains than Bill, but more money," "I believe in discipline," "I'm not that kind of a girl," etc. Furthermore, it was pointed out earlier that the self-concept is an *organized* configuration of perceptions of the self. This fact may be represented in a diagram in which the self-concept is shown as a regular geometrical figure. This is to indicate that we all feel that we make sense to ourselves — that we have some kind of internal organization and integrity — even if to others we seem to make no sense at all. The fact of organization is of enormous importance, because it means that it is difficult for all of us to change one aspect of our beliefs or attitudes without having to rearrange our entire self-organization.

The self-concept, then, is the fundamental determinant of all our behavior. Indeed, since it is an organization of our past experiences and perceptions as well as of our values and goals, it determines the character of the reality we see. Each individual has his own and unique way of extracting meaning from the world about him. For example, an industrial engineer may submit a plan — let us call it Plan X — which has for him the meaning "increased production." He looks expectantly to his colleagues for approval. But to his colleagues Plan X can have entirely different meanings, each looking at the plan from his own frame of reference: "This plan means no more production than before," "This means that my Plan Y will be ditched if I don't put up a fight," "Plan X reduces my job to being a mere flunky around here," "Plan X is my chance for promotion," "Plan X may increase production, but who wants to increase production at this time?"

11 The industrial engineer who has proposed Plan X feels that its advantages are so clear and obvious that they ought to be plain to everybody. Encountering unexpected opposition, he is at once tempted to think of his opponents as foolish, stupid, misguided, or wilfully obdurate. If, however, we think in terms of the self-concept and the way in which each individual must of necessity see the world from his own frame of reference, it is obvious at once that each person who objects to Plan X objects to it for reasons that make perfectly good sense to him, even if they don't make sense to the industrial engineer. Let me put this observation in the form of a principle, namely, that "everything we do seems to be reasonable and necessary at the time we are doing it" (Snygg and Combs, *Individual Behavior,* p. 12). The following incident will illustrate the principle:

> Several years ago (the writer) was driving a car at dusk along a western road. A globular mass about two feet in diameter appeared suddenly in the path of the car. A passenger in the front seat screamed and grasped the wheel, attempting to steer the car around the object. The driver tightened his grip and drove directly into it.
>
> In each case the behavior of the individual was determined by his own phenomenal field. The passenger, an Easterner, saw the object in the highway as a boulder and fought desperately to steer the car around it. The driver, a native of the vicinity, saw it as tumbleweed and devoted his efforts to keeping his passenger from overturning the car. (p. 14)

From the point of view of the driver, the passenger was acting "insanely"; so, from the point of view of the passenger, was the driver. But each was trying only to do what seemed to him at the moment "reasonable and necessary." Each had only his own way of interpreting what he saw, based on his past experiences.

We subscribe to magazines that we agree with because they fortify our self-concept; opposition magazines we find threatening to our self-concept and therefore distasteful. Whether or not we accept a dinner invitation revolves around whether or not we find the idea of associating with the people who invited us enhancing to our self-concept. And since the self-concept includes predictions about ourselves as well as the organization of past experiences, we select or avoid new situations according to our own predictions as to our ability to handle them. If we feel that our organization will be seriously disturbed or threatened by the new situation, we will avoid it.

One last point about the self-concept before we return to the subject of communication. The self-concept tends to rigidify under threat. If we think of ourselves as "intelligent," and other people or an unfortunate set of circumstances offer the implication that we are "unintelligent," we assert our belief in our intelligence with redoubled force. The individual who is unsure of his right to his self-concept tends especially to hold it rigidly. Let us say that there is a salesman whose self-concept is "I am the best salesman in the company." Let us say that the facts are otherwise; several other salesmen are surpassing him. It is possible for such an individual to maintain his self-concept rigidly in spite of mounting evidence, fortifying himself by whatever rationalizations he can think up: "They're giving me the worst territory," "I'd have a terrific record if I could bring myself to descend to the methods some of the other fellows are using," etc.

Communicative frustration

So we return now to the problem of communication. At what point do we become deeply concerned about communication? Usually it is at the point when we feel a severe sense of frustration because the message we want to communicate is not getting across. If we are on the management end, we may say, "Our employees have got to learn . . ." If we represent the union, we say, "Management has simply got to realize . . ." If we are parents, we say, "It's high time Wilbur understood . . ." If we are talking about international relations, we say, "The point must be made clear to the Russians . . ."

What fascinates me about this condition of communicative frustration is the psychological condition on both sides. Mr. A has tried to tell something to Mr. B. Mr. B., because he does not like the content of the message as he understands it, or because he does not like the tone of voice in which it was delivered, finds some kind of threat to his self-esteem in the message and resists it — by ignoring it, by arguing back, and often by seeming to twist its meaning in the course of arguing back. Each time Mr. A repeats his message — perhaps getting it down to words of one syllable, perhaps shouting it in a louder tone of voice, or both — Mr. B's resistance increases until his attitude becomes quite rigid.

But Mr. B's resistance implies a criticism of Mr. A's message, and hence of Mr. A himself. Mr. A feels therefore quite threatened by this resistance, and he too becomes rigid. Because Mr. A too has his self-concept, it is much easier for him to think, "My God, this fellow B is stupid," than to think, "Maybe there's something wrong with my message or my way of trying to communicate it." Rapidly the situation develops into "communicative deadlock," in which each is threatened by the attitude of the other,

13 and therefore each is rigidly defensive of his own views. This condition is easily recognized. Whenever you hear the expression, "Give him an inch and he'll take a mile," you know that there is communicative deadlock. A dramatic example in recent history was the truce negotiation at Panmunjom, where the deadlock continued for months, and where the felt threat on each side was enormous.

Non-evaluative listening

But let us go back, in search for a paradigm with which to explore the problems raised by the attitudes of mutual paranoia on both sides of the Iron Curtain, to Mr. A and Mr. B. Can the communicative deadlock between Mr. A and Mr. B ever be removed? Of course it can — and that is what psychiatry and clinical psychology are all about. And we can learn something about the unblocking of communication especially from the successful application of psychotherapeutic theories in, for example, business management. An important approach is that which Dr. Carl Rogers calls "non-evaluative listening."

In brief, non-evaluative listening amounts to this: assuming you are Mr. A, and you have tried in vain to convince Mr. B of an idea or proposal, and Mr. B, his defenses thoroughly aroused, doggedly resists, it does no good for you to continue to shout and pound the table. What you must do is something entirely different, namely, temporarily suspend your purposes and listen to Mr. B — and listen non-evaluatively. Such listening means listening without argument or passing judgment, listening fully in order to understand thoroughly how the problem looks to Mr. B and why Mr. B's resistance makes sense to him, given the kind and amount of information he possesses, given the goals for which he is striving.

What happens to Mr. B if you listen non-evaluatively to him is that, no longer confronted with the necessity of countering your arguments, he begins to relax the rigidity of his defense. His defensive utterances give way to informative utterances. He begins to tone down the absoluteness of his statements, to be less stereotyped and propagandistic in his responses.

Communication being a process of interaction, something also begins to happen to you. Because Mr. B is making less extreme statements, you yourself are less threatened by his remarks, and your own defenses begin to relax. Having entered emphatically into his view of the world, you may succeed in coming to the conclusion that his views, while still unacceptable, at least make a certain amount of sense, given his assumptions. Perhaps this is the turning point in the interactional situation — the point at which you begin to acknowledge that Mr. B is neither dishonest nor insane — and that he seemed so largely because he started with different assumptions and therefore different perceptions of the world. I say this is the turning point, because this is the point at which you are willing to admit Mr. B into the human race.

The next possibility is that Mr. B, having been listened to, may now be willing to listen, and to listen non-defensively and therefore without distorting your message to fit into his hostile preconceptions of your purposes. And as you state your views, more calmly than you had been stating them earlier, you will moderate the dogmatism of your own presentation and further reduce the reasons for his defensiveness.

Then, since both you and Mr. B have tried seriously to listen, you will have received information from him which you formerly did not have; he too will have acquired information which was news to him. In the light of this new knowledge possessed by both of you, both your original proposal and his resistance to it may be obsolete. You jointly are able, at this point, to work out a new scheme which takes into account the entire body of new information — a solution that will be satisfactory to both. I am not speaking here of compromise, which is a matter of bargaining from fixed positions to one in between. In two-way communication such as I have been talking about, both sides acquire new information so that formerly fixed positions no longer exist, and a resolution is found on new grounds and at different levels. It is this emergence of novelty as the result of communication that makes the students of psychotherapy, the students of group dynamics, the counseling profession, and the general semanticists so hopeful of the possibility that they may be able to contribute something to the solution of the big problems of conflict resolution that confront us today.

Therapeutic effect of successful communication

In short, successful communication is therapeutic in effect, whether we think of psychotherapy narrowly as applied to the psychiatrist and his patient, or broadly as applied to the clearing up of misunderstandings and delusions that becloud relationships between people in normal business and family contacts. In this broad sense of psychotherapy in which no psychiatrist is involved, there is a general answer, namely, that since listening is at the heart of psychotherapy whoever has the emotional strength and the courage to begin listening to the other fellow instead of shouting at him can be the psychotherapist for the other. Hence, the emotionally secure mother can act as psychotherapist for the child, but the emotionally strong child can also act as psychotherapist for an upset mother. The general rule then is this: whether you are parent or child, employer or employee, teacher or student, art director or artist, if you yourself have the firmness and security of internal organization to listen patiently to the other fellow, even when you feel that you know he is wrong, you can start the psychotherapeutic process rolling.

But a good listener does not merely remain silent. He asks questions. However, these questions must avoid all implications (whether in tone of voice or in wording) of skepticism or challenge or hostility. They must be clearly motivated by curiosity about the speaker's views. Such questions, which may be called "questions for clarification," usually take the form, "Would you expand on that point about . . . ?" "Would you mind restating that argument about . . . ?" "What exactly is your recommendation again?" Perhaps the most useful kind of question at this stage is something like, "I am going to restate in my words what I think you mean. Then would you mind telling me if I've understood you correctly?"

Questions of uniqueness

The late Dr. Irving J. Lee of Northwestern University has suggested another form of questioning which he describes as "the request for information concerning the uniqueness of the particular characteristics of the condition or proposal under consideration." I shall simply call these questions "questions of uniqueness." All too often, we tend to listen to a speaker or his speech in terms of a generalization, "Oh he's just another of those progressive educators," "Isn't that just like a commercial designer?" "That's the familiar Robjohn-Giddings approach," "That's the old Bauhaus pitch," etc. It is a curious and dangerous fact — dangerous to communication, that is — that once we classify a speech in this way, we stop listening, because, as we say, "We've heard that stuff before." But *this* speech by *this* individual at *this* time and place is a *particular* event, while the "that stuff" with which we are classifying this speech is a generalization from the past. Questions of uniqueness are designed to prevent what might be called the functional deafness which we induce in ourselves by reacting to speakers and their speeches in terms of the generalizations we apply to them. Questions of uniqueness take such forms as these: "How large is the firm you work for, and do they make more than one product?" "Exactly what kind of synthetic plastic did you use on that project?" "Are your remarks on abstract expressionism and Jackson Pollock intended to apply equally to the work of De Kooning?"

16 Something else that needs to be watched is the habit of over-generalizing from the speaker's remarks. If a speaker is critical of, let us say, the way in which design is taught at a particular school, some persons in the audience seem automatically to assume that the speaker is saying that design shouldn't be taught at all. When I speak on the neglected art of listening, as I have done on other occasions at other places, I usually am confronted with the question, "If everybody listened, who would do the talking?" This type of misunderstanding may be called the "pickling in brine fallacy," after the senior Oliver Wendell Holmes' famous remark, "Just because I say I like sea bathing, that doesn't mean I want to be pickled in brine." When Alfred Korzybski found himself being misunderstood in this way, he used to assert with special forcefulness, "I say what I say; I do not say what I do not say." Questions of uniqueness, properly chosen, prevent not only the questioner but everyone else present from projecting into a speaker's remarks meanings that were not intended.

All too often, the fact that misunderstanding exists is not apparent until deeper misunderstandings have already occurred because of the original one. We have all had the experience of being at meetings or at social gatherings at which Mr. X says something, Mr. Y believes Mr. X to have said something quite different and argues against what he believes Mr. X to have said. Then Mr. X, not understanding Mr. Y's objections (which may be legitimate objections to what Mr. X didn't say), defends his original statement with further statements. These further statements, interpreted by Mr. Y in the light of mistaken assumptions, lead to further mistaken assumptions, which in turn induce in Mr. X mistaken assumptions about Mr. Y. In a matter of minutes, the discussion is a dozen miles away from the original topic. Thereafter it can take from 20 minutes to two hours to untangle the mess and restore the discussion to a consideration of Mr. X's original point. This is the kind of time-wasting which I should like to help avoid.

It is not to say that I expect or wish this or any conference to avoid argument. But let us argue about what has been said, and not about what has not been said. And let us discuss not for victory but for clarification. If we do so, we shall find, I believe, that ultimately agreement and disagreement, approval and disapproval, are not very important after all. The important thing is to come away from the conference with a fund of information — information about what other people are doing and thinking and why. It is only as we fully understand directions other than our own and the reasons for them that we better understand our own place in the

17 scheme of things. Which is but another way of saying that while the result of communications successfully imparted is a self-satisfaction, the result of communications successfully received is self-insight.

The parable of "Red Eye"

I should like to draw these remarks to a close by referring to a parable. This parable is completely unsound as archeology, anthropology, or history, but I guarantee that it is a good parable — I wrote it myself. Its title is "Red Eye and the Woman Problem."

Once, long ago, tens of thousands of years before history began, people were worried, as they have often been since, about the chaotic condition of their lives. For in those days men took by force the women they desired. There was no way of stopping them.

If you wanted a woman but found that she was already the partner of another man, all you needed to do was to kill him and drag her home. Naturally, someone else might slug you a little later to get her away from you, but that was the chance you took if you wanted a woman at all.

Consequently, there wasn't much of what you could call family life. The men were too busy suspiciously watching each other. And time that might have been spent fishing or hunting or otherwise increasing the general standard of living was wasted in constant and anxious measures to defend one's woman.

Many people saw that this was no way for human beings to live. As they said among themselves: "Truly we are strange creatures. In some ways we are highly civilized. We no longer eat raw flesh, as did our savage ancestors. Our technical men have perfected stone arrowheads and powerful bows so that we can slay the fastest deer that runs. Our medicine men can foretell the running of fish in the streams, and our sorcerers drive away illnesses. At the Institute for Advanced Studies at Notecnirp, a group of bright young men are said to be working out a dance that will make the rain fall. Little by little, we are mastering the secrets of nature, so that we are able to live like civilized men and not like beasts."

"Yet," they continued, "we have not mastered ourselves. There are those among us who continue to snatch women away from each other by force, so that every man of necessity lives in fear of his fellows. People agree, of course, that all this killing ought to be stopped. But no one is stopping it. The most fundamental of human problems, that of securing a mate and bringing up one's children under some kind of decent, orderly system, remains unsolved. Unless we can find some way of placing the

18 man-woman relationship on a decent and human basis, our pretensions to civilization are hollow."

For many generations the thoughtful men of the tribe pondered this problem. How could men and women, living peacefully together with their children, be protected from the lusts of the few, who went around killing other men in order to possess their women?

Slowly, and only after centuries of groping discussion, they evolved an answer. They proposed that men and women who have decided to live together permanently be bound by a "contract," by which they meant the uttering, before the priests of the tribe, of solemn promises, binding on their future behavior. This contract was to be known as "marriage." The man in the marriage was to be known as a "husband," the woman as a "wife."

They further proposed that this contract was to be observed and honored by all the people of the tribe. In other words, if a given woman, Slendershanks, was known to be the "wife" of a given man, Beetlebrow, everyone in the tribe was to agree not to molest their domestic arrangements. Futhermore, they proposed that if anyone failed to respect this contract and killed another man to possess his "wife," he was to be punished by the collective force of tribal authority.

In order to put these proposals into effect, a great conference was called, and delegates arrived from all branches of the tribe. Some came with glad hearts, filled with the hope that humanity was about to enter a new era. Some came with faint hearts, not expecting much to come out of the conference, but feeling that it was at least worth a try. Some came simply because they had been elected delegates and were getting their expenses paid; they were willing to go along with whomever proved to be in the majority.

All the time the conference was going on, however, a big, backward savage called Red-Eye the Atavism, who was so loud-mouthed that he always had a following in spite of his unprepossessing personality, kept shouting scornful remarks from the sidelines. He called the delegates "visionaries," "eggheads," "impractical theorists," "starry-eyed dreamers," "crackpots," and "panty-waists." He gleefully pointed out that many of the delegates had themselves been, at an earlier date, woman-snatchers. (This, unfortunately, was true — which didn't help the conference any.)

He shouted to Hairy Hands, who was one of the delegates, "You can't think Brawny Legs is going to leave your woman alone just because he makes an agreement, do you?" And he shouted to Brawny Legs, "You don't think Hairy Hands is going to leave your woman alone just because he makes an agreement, do you?" And he poured derision on all the delegates, referring to their discussion as "striped pants kind of talk, like who ever heard of 'husband,' and 'wife,' and 'marriage' and all that double-dome Choctaw!"

Then Red-Eye the Atavism turned to his following, the crowd of timid and tiny-minded people who always found their self-assurance in the loudness of his voice and he yelled, "Look at those damn fool delegates, will you? They think they can change human nature!"

Thereupon the crowd rolled over with laughter and repeated after him, "Haw, haw! They think they can change human nature!"

That broke up the conference. It was another two thousand years, therefore, before marriage was finally instituted in that tribe — two thousand years during which innumerable men were killed defending their women, two thousand years during which men who had no designs on their neighbor's women killed each other as a precaution against being killed themselves (this was known as "preventive war"), two thousand years during which the arts of peace languished, two thousand years during which people despaired as they dreamed of a distant future time when a man might live with the woman of his choice without arming himself to the teeth and watching over her day and night.

Perhaps you find this parable depressing. Whether or not you find it so depends on what you abstract from it as the most important point. Red Eye the Atavism, it is true, scored a big victory on that occasion. But it is also true that marriage (however imperfect an institution *that* may be) was finally instituted.

But as for the big problem of threatened international violence with which we are now confronted, we don't have two thousand years to find the institutional solution. Indeed, we don't have two hundred years — nor even 20 years — perhaps not even two.

And that's our problem.

COMMENTS BY DR. HAYAKAWA IN ANSWER TO QUESTIONS

If people's self and self-concept are all different, and if advertising must appeal to a common denominator in a mass market, have any studies been made of common denominators among different self-concepts?

The question is whether, for purposes of advertising, studies have been made of self-concepts and the common features in self-concepts of many people so that you can address advertising to large groups of people at once.

In fact, is that not quite what you ordinarily do in a lot of your r′ search? Perhaps you use other terminology for it? I just don't know.

When you specify, and say let's shoot for the teenage market or the young marrieds or whatever group, don't you have a kind of definition of the group's self-concept of teenagers or the young marrieds that you are aiming towards? Do you do this in anything other than in an intuitive way or do you have some research to back you up in defining how the teenage mind works? I think that you do have a pretty systematic inquiry into these matters.

Every individual's self-concept is ultimately unique, but certainly there are common features in many, many self-concepts, because we have common needs after all.

Doesn't the common denominator apply to terms such as love, hate, fear, patriotism?

It could very well be. Certainly love, hate, fear, patriotism — all of these emotions are partly self-concepts, there is no question about that.

How would you talk to "Red-Eye" Khrushchev, if you had the opportunity as a delegate for the U.S., to get this man to listen to reason?

You know Theodore Roosevelt's famous dictum, "Speak softly and carry a big stick," is very important. I want to emphasize the "speak softly" part of it. This is a very important part of it. That is, if we are not trying to pick the fight. Then, there is every reason to speak softly and to take advantage of whatever little threads of communication that can be established between us and the Soviet Union, whether it be an exchange of ballet troupes, pianists, of scientific journals, or hockey teams.

By the way, emerging literature behind the "Iron Curtain" shows that they have the same problem. What should socialist advertising do different from that of a dirty capitalistic society? You find that they have to do the very same things. Anyway, in this field you can provide the Soviet advertiser with technical help. There are all sorts of tiny threads which can be established, which may make it unnecessary to use that "big stick" ultimately.

I would like to use the analogy of the threads because a thread is a very, very weak thing, but great heavy ropes are made from lots and lots of tiny threads.

Is there not a personality where the individual's self-concept is a fluctuating thing, changing from time to time?

A normal self-concept on the part of a healthy individual should be changing from time to time because, after all, in a given moment of time you are 35, and then eventually you are 45, and eventually you are 55, and you cannot maintain the same self-concept through all that time.

Also your relationships with others — at one time you are assistant manager, and later you are manager, and later you are fired. So if we can maintain a flexible self-concept, organized properly at the various levels, then we are all right.

One of the most interesting things, and this is Carl Rogers' theory about it, is that after people successfully complete psychotherapy there are certain external signs of it. You can see that there is a self-concept reorganization change going on, which is manifested by certain changes in dress. Men begin to wear louder ties. Women begin to pay attention to certain features of dress that they were permitting to go ignored for a long time. So that changing self-concept is normally to be expected.

Let me give you the opposite case, to go back to "Death of a Salesman." His trouble was his self-concept did not change with the years as circumstances changed, and therefore he had to progress and vacate himself more and more in order to maintain that certain self-concept. That is the danger.

Have you been able to keep up with that field of technology where man is trying to communicate with his machines — specifically computers and language machines — and do you find any of the principles there?

The answer to that is like talking about the self-concept. I gave you an example of the kid who defines himself as not good at mathematics. Well, that's me. This whole machine translation — this computer business, which involves an awful lot of mathematics — that's not for me. I couldn't possibly understand that stuff, so I really haven't followed it very much. But there are certain features of machine computers that fascinate me very much.

Some people feed problems into machines and sit back to wait for the answers. When the answers come back they stand in astonishment, as if the oracle had spoken, or almost as if the voice had come from God himself — because this had come from the I.B.M. machine. They seem to forget that it was *they* who fed the machine to give that answer. The idea of an I.B.M. machine projecting a kind of God-like emission is getting more and more widespread.

This reminds me of a short story by Ben Hecht; it was also made into a movie. It was about a man, a ventriloquist, who had a dummy, and the dummy kept talking back to him. He would quarrel with his dummy, there were furious quarrels every night. The ventriloquist had an assistant, a pretty girl, and he became more and more convinced that this dummy was making passes at this girl. One night, in a fit of jealousy, he hacked the dummy to pieces, and then for the rest of his life he had to hide out from the police. This man was known as the Great Gobel, that was the name of the story, that was the name of the ventriloquist.

I have begun to feel that some people are acting like the Great Gobel as regards their I.B.M. machines.

When are you going to start a school similar to the Famous Artists Schools?

Actually, in a sense, we have one now. At San Francisco State College, we give adult seminars constantly — sometimes one-week seminars, sometimes evening seminars. If you will drop me a note about it, I can get you the information. Actually, there are many, many people who are interested in semantics, group dynamics and fields like this, who do conduct workshops of this kind. The University of Chicago has a home study course in general semantics which I guarantee — because I wrote the course.

I believe that you edit a magazine. Where is this published?

The editorial and business offices of *ETC.* are at San Francisco State College. It is a quarterly magazine on general semantics. I started the magazine 19 years ago, and I have kept it going all these years as a sort of unpaid labor of love. Someone has to do this sort of thing, in a scholarly field — to get it started and keep it going. So I have no compunction in asking you to subscribe. It is $4.00 a year. Send it to *ETC.* at San Francisco State College.

thoughts on film

SAUL BASS

Editor's Note: At the Conference, Saul Bass showed a number of his films including, as he pointed out, "some of the in-process material that I am working on at the moment . . . risking exposure of the half-finished thing in the interest of whatever insight it might give us to the visual communication process."

We are therefore reproducing here only Mr. Bass' comments in answer to questions, in the belief that this "dialogue" will contribute to an appreciation of some of the elements of communicating in filmic terms.

How much of a picture do you see or how much of an idea do they give you about a picture before you sit down to work up what you do there?

I usually will either read the script, watch it being shot or participate in the shooting before I go to work. It is very rare that I will be brought into a film after it has been done, although that will happen occasionally.

More often than not I am brought into the situation at very early stages. That is important aside from its desirability from the creative point of view. In the case of "Big Country," for example, it would not have been possible to get the material I wanted if I had been brought in after the picture was shot. I got these shots with a second unit — while they were on location at Stockton, with the whole company. It would have been far too costly if the

THE BIG COUNTRY

stagecoach, horses, and everything else were not already there. But it was relatively simple to do in a few days of shooting under the circumstances.

As I look at the "Big Country" title I am reminded of a little problem we had while shooting it. Part of my intent in the title was to keep the stagecoach very small, and all the closeups very large, in order to achieve the most extreme scale. It was also desirable to have huge dust clouds raised by the coach, so that the concept of the shot would be an unfolding dust cloud, rather than a moving stagecoach. However, it had just rained a few days before we shot, and there was no dust. In sheer desperation we went into Stockton, and got a load of flour in sacks, and we had a man sitting in the back of the coach dumping the flour as the coach went along.

How do you work with the people who compose the music for the score?

That is a very important part of the whole process. I work very closely with the composers, and there is a very close integration between the sound and the image.

It works in various ways. Since the title must reflect the character of the film, the music for the title usually comes out of the music for the film as a whole. Its particular expression in relation to the title grows out of collaboration between the composer and myself. In the course of this we discuss what my imagery is going to be like, and we fix points at which certain kinds of things have to happen in order for the audio and visual to bind.

Then he works independently on his music, while I work independently on my film, and at the point at which I have my rough cut, we may lay in a rough soundtrack consisting of one or two instruments just to see how it sounds, and then adjust further. I may adjust in cutting or timing, and he may adjust in other ways musically. This is the way it develops.

One curious experience I had, oddly enough, was on the title I did for "The Man with the Golden Arm," many years ago, with Elmer Bernstein doing the music. Elmer and I did not confer with each other while this was going on. The only thing both of us knew, was that we had a beat to work to. He was working his music to a beat, and I was working my image to a beat. The first time we experienced image and sound it came together beautifully. Apparently all that was necessary, in that case, to unite us was the beat. Of course, having a fine piece of music helps.

Do you work up your special effects on storyboard before you go into production?

That is a very interesting question, because I had to revise my entire way of working as I got more deeply into the live-action aspects of film work.

WALK ON THE WILD SIDE

27 You see, in animation, you can truly predict what is going to happen, because you draw it. And what you draw is duplicated by people who translate this into a number of cells, and they can make it move precisely the way you want it to move. You can have exact control from beginning to end.

The live-action image is not so susceptible to complete pre-visualization, as I'm sure many of you have discovered when you work with photography. It is one thing to make your layout, and render what the camera is supposed to see. When you get out on the set, a lot of things happen that you didn't predict, and opportunities present themselves that you couldn't envision on a drawing board.

So, I found that it was wise to proceed in a different way in developing live-action material. Once I have a concept, I shoot footage. I go out with a camera and shoot the stuff in experimental form, and find out what's going to happen. For instance, in the case of "Walk on the Wild Side" we shot experimental footage in 16mm and still form . . . and then made up the storyboard.

Incidentally, it was my wife's little cat, Tippy-Tu, that we used as our subject for "Walk on the Wild Side" in order to find out how a cat moved, how a cat "feels," and how a cat looks on film. All of this footage was based upon that cat, and was a duplication of what we got on 16mm film with him. Unfortunately, he died between the time we shot the experimental footage and when we were ready to go into production. So, we were unable to actually use Tippy-Tu, who was a fantastic actor and did exactly what he was asked to do as though he truly understood . . . which he did.

But the cat that we shot in production was most strongly opposed to the whole idea and I had to develop the patience of a Buddha to get this footage. We shot for about five days. The first day we got 90 percent of the footage that may be seen in the title, and we sat around after that waiting for the cat to do a few other things, which he never did. He wouldn't walk, he wouldn't sit — no matter how we asked him to do so. I learned that there are no "trained" cats. They have trained dogs. But all animal trainers refer to cats as "working" cats, which means when they feel like it, they work.

I was up on a traveling boom with the cameraman, since we had to catch the cat as he was moving. The cat was put down — we started to move — presumably the cat was to start walking. But soon the cameraman was frantically yelling "Where is the cat?" We were moving, but the cat wasn't. He was sitting just where he had been put down. And so it went.

How long have film titles been a separate business? Has it always been such?

You must understand that film titles have always been with us. There are organizations in Hollywood that are geared to turn out only film titles, and have been doing this for many years. So that it is really a separate activity and always has been. I think what you are referring to is, how long have they been given more attention? I would say, just in recent years. I just think it is an area that has not been fully understood, and the opportunities presented have not been utilized. I have tried in the titles I have done to exploit these opportunities.

In a film, as in any theatrical presentation, the first few moments are a very important part of the performance. This is understood quite well in theatre. In film, for some strange reason, the presentation of credits has always been considered as separate from the story proper. My view of the matter is that the credits are a part of the tale.

I should also indicate that I recognize that credits are a very serious and actual trade requirement. People who work in film will often depend to some measurable degree upon the fact that their association with certain aspects of the film is noted and observed in a trade sense. Frequently, their future employment may be related to that observation by others in the field.

However, there is a curious contradiction in the situation. While the credits are terribly important and have great interest for those who work in film and in related fields, in the larger sense there is absolutely no interest in this on the part of the broad spectrum of people that make up the film audience. I would say that they are interested in the important stars; they knew about a De Mille; they know about a Sam Goldwyn; they are familiar with an Alfred Hitchcock — and there are a few others.

So you have a situation where there is a whole three minutes or more of "stuff" at the beginning of a film that is usually expendable. It's time when popcorn is bought, small talk is exchanged, and various urgencies are accommodated . . . and then the film begins.

It is my view that these are very important moments. It is the beginning . . . and a part of the story. An atmosphere has to be created for what is to come. This is the approach I have taken to the handling of film titles. I try to satisfy both worlds: the world that wants to read the names, and the world that wants to feel the story. It is sometimes very difficult. I don't always succeed. I have been criticized for, perhaps, submerging the names. But I honestly try to "do right" by them.

lenses by PANAVISION
SPARTACUS
music composed
ALEX NORTH

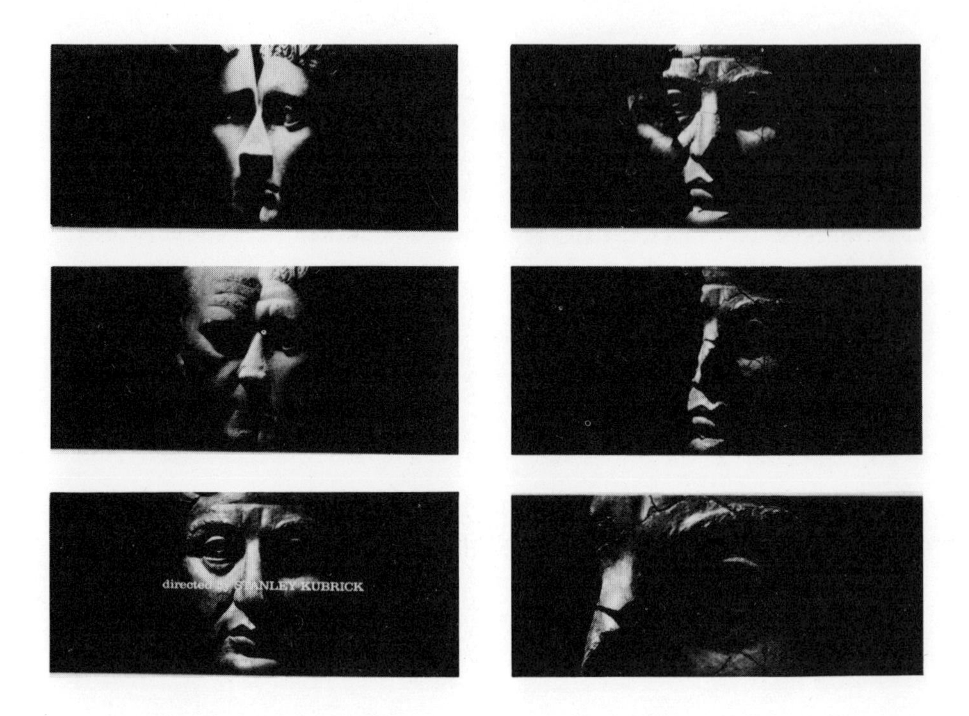

In certain of your credits, you are listed as a visual consultant. Exactly what does that apply to?

In the last few years, I have been asked by several directors and producers to work on the film as a whole, and this has taken various forms. I worked on "Spartacus" in this way, and Hitchcock's film "Psycho," and on "West Side Story." I did different things in relation to each film. In the case of "Spartacus," aside from the title, I designed among other things, a battle and a major set. In the case of "Psycho" I designed, for instance, the Janet Leigh murder sequence. Between that and a few other things I am working on, I seem to be immersing myself in mayhem. That's the way it goes sometimes.

How closely do you work with the art director on a motion picture? What is his sphere of influence? Where does his sphere of influence stop and yours begin?

Well, the function of the art director in a film is quite different from that which is normal for an art director in relation to advertising. In advertising, the *art director* is responsible for the visual form of the ad. In film, the *director* is responsible for the visual expression of the film — he is the designer of the film. He frames the shot, selects the angle, sets the scene, determines whether or not the camera will move and how it will move. The art director, the cameraman and others implement his directions. My work in relation to the production aspects of the film is more closely allied to that of the director.

These categorical delineations however are often meaningless. William Cameron Menzies, credited as art director for "Gone With the Wind," was really a Second Unit director who was responsible for conceiving and designing some of the most magnificent shots in that film. Yet there are art directors whose activity centers around architecture and interior decoration.

During the time of your employment with some of the agencies in New York, and before you started designing for films, there came a change about you. What prompted your decision to go into film designing?

I never know how to tackle a question like this. I mean to say that if I were to really answer it I would have to say things like: "I got out of the agency field because I felt it was restrictive; because the basic character of agency structure tends to mitigate against creativity and innovation; because I wanted to choose my clients and my problems, and not inherit them." I admire the people who are attempting to reverse the process. I think there are a few wonderful agencies that manage to do it. How? I don't know. But they manage to maintain a fine level of work. I found that I was not happy, and could not do the things I wanted to do within the agency structure as I saw it at that time, so I free-lanced.

How I got into film was simply pure accident. I just happened to be somewhere where a film was being made. Otto Preminger, when making the film "Carmen Jones," asked me to design a symbol for it, which I did. You may recall that the symbol consisted of a rose and a flame. One day, we said, "Wouldn't it be great if we'd put it up on the screen in front of the film." He liked the idea. I liked the idea. So I did it.

And that started me. It was film, and it moved. I was flabbergasted by the movement.

In making the title I had the thought that, if we could shoot the flame so that it would truly separate with intertwining forms, it would make a very exciting moving image. I seemed to recall seeing a photograph in a magazine once which had this kind of flame where the forms of the flame actually intertwined like strands of cord or rope. I drove the technicians mad trying to get this. After repeated failures, I scoured my library one day for this photograph which I was going to triumphantly bring to the technicians to show them. I discovered, when I found it, that it was a shot of water coming out of a faucet which had been turned upside down. But fortunately, by that time, the flame began to look the way I wanted it to look . . . so I quietly put the book away.

Reminiscing about this period reminds me of a title I made at about the same time for a film called "The Racers." My design for this film called for a racing flag which fluttered in the breeze. The film opened on about three squares of the flag, and then was to pull back very sharply to reveal a hand holding the flag. Now, I had done little live-action shooting until then, so when I was asked by the producer to be on the set on Tuesday morning I thought he wanted me there to observe — which I was very glad to do. There was quite a crew on hand to make the shot. They got all set up and organized, and the next thing I knew somebody turned to me (I didn't know he was the assistant director) and said, "Are you ready, Mr. Bass?" I said, "I'm ready." The next thing I heard was that characteristic cadence of sounds which follows a director's signal to proceed . . . and I realized that *I* was the director. Now, I thought, If I am the director, then I want to really get into it. So I put myself on the camera dolly which was on a set of tracks. "I'd like to see this pull-back before you take it." I stood on the platform, crouched down, hands on knees and head to camera sight. "Okay, let's see it." So they went . . . "whap!" And I went . . . "whap!" . . . right into the camera.

And there I was with my head in the camera, trying to look like that's the way *I* do it.

design and management

RALPH E. ECKERSTROM
Director of Design, Advertising and Public Relations, Container Corporation of America

In any corporation it is the relationship of design and management which holds the key to the realization of the potential of good design for favorably influencing a corporation's success.

Walter Paepcke, the founder of Container Corporation and our late chairman of the board, built the first International Design Conference in Aspen in 1950 around the subject "Design as a Function of Management." Prior to the date by 15 years, he had established the company's Department of Design. He, along with Adriano Olivetti, who had an even more comprehensive design program for his company, provided the entry of design and esthetics to the councils of corporation management. Design, for the first time, was given an opportunity to prove its worth to a business enterprise on a broad and integrated basis.

Happily, both Container and Olivetti have been reasonably successful. Though the exact contribution of design cannot be proven, I doubt that there are many who do not recognize that the visual image which each of these companies has presented has had some favorable effect on the success of their products and on these corporations as a whole.

"Design as a Function of Management" seemed like a great idea to Walter Paepcke. It pointed out to corporation management that a product or a package or an advertisement which fits the designer's criteria of "good design" is, in fact, a more saleable product or package and, in advertising, a more effective piece of communication. *Point this out,* and management will certainly become vitally interested in "good design." Interested management would respond by seeking out the best, the most creative designers and art directors, and give them the freedom and the responsibility for the development of "good design."

Operating under this concept, managements and designers would become partners in the projection of unique, tasteful, exciting, esthetically satisfying, and *sales stimulating* products, packages and advertisements.

The factor of "measurement"

With few exceptions, this concept never got off the ground. It never really got off the ground because there is one apparently unbridgeable chasm between management and design. This is the factor of measurement. Management demands measurement, mass production and marketing demand measurement — units per hour, costs per unit, man hours, number of persons, cost per person reached, ratings, market surveys and analyses.

Measurements such as these provide the criteria for the evaluation of management itself. For, in the final analysis, the shareholders of a company measure management's success or failure by the company's profit or loss.

To many designers, these measurements are anathema. The creative person does not want his creative expression measured on what, to him, is an arbitrary scale of values. In fact, the esthetic expression for the creator, or the viewer of it, is beyond measurement on these terms — for the esthetic experience means an experience that is enjoyed for itself alone. Designers want measurement based on the irrational criterion of enjoyment. Management demands measurement on the rational criterion of dollars and cents.

The split between management and designers over the need for measurement and the criteria for measurement is evidenced in the designers' and art directors' annual exhibitions. These exhibitions of packaging and advertising art are made up of work which is selected almost solely on the basis of its esthetic characteristics. Rarely is a reference made to the esthetic quality of the advertisements from the designer's or art director's point of view and *its relationship to the selling ability* of the advertisement from management's point of view. In these *art directors'* selections, the basic reason for the very existence of the advertisement is seldom considered.

In other words, there is no measurement of the advertisement's effect on the sales of the product or service.

Illustrative of this is one of the stories that have come down to us about the great Knute Rockne days at Notre Dame. Rockne decided that his football players should play soccer in the off-season to keep in shape. He called the team together one afternoon and explained his idea, but his explanation of how the game of soccer is played put more stress on the body contact aspects of it than on finesse. Finally, he sent the trainer into the locker room to get a soccer ball. At this point, one rough, tough Irishman growled: "The hell with the ball, let's start the game."

All too often, that's the way it is when the designer starts his work these days. All too often, that's the way many of these exhibitions look to management — the ad was brilliantly designed and executed only to be lost because the basic selling idea wasn't carried with it.

The result is that management ignores or makes light of these exhibitions because they know that there is no planned correlation between the advertisement's solution and its selling power. Therefore, except for the momentary prestige which an art award might bring them, these exhibitions are of little significance to managements.

In passing, I might add that even for the design profession these shows have relaxed into a cliché of acceptance and recognition.

In its zeal for designing for "design's sake," the design profession cuts itself off from management and thereby from the realities of business. By so doing, not only is the capability and the power of good design largely unused but, in addition and even more importantly, business and society as a whole do not reflect or have the substantial benefits of the high standard of design which is possible.

Let's move now from the designer's present inability to relate his work satisfactorily to the criteria of measurement that business requires, to the inability of business to understand the unmeasurable, irrational aspects of design.

The advantage of artistic creativity

Let us take the problem facing management of the stultifying basic similarity of competing products. In a competitive system such as ours, where the same basic materials are available to all manufacturers, where essentially the same equipment and production methods are used throughout an industry, and where dissemination of knowledge makes every technological innovation subject to immediate imitation, the only real advantage one company may have over its competitors is its resources for artistic creativity.

Management should be limited only by the creative ability of their designers and *their* parallel creativity in the judgment of these ideas. The result, in a hotly contested competitive race, may well mean success or failure for the company.

It is paradoxical that management has a fear or hesitancy in trying the unconventional, even while every company is apparently seeking that unique idea in product, package or promotion which will provide it with a competitive advantage.

Does management realize that the unique idea in product, package, or promotion can be the result of creativity which is essentially their own private property? Apparently, so far as the product itself is concerned, they do. Industry has claimed the skills of science for this purpose. The widespread establishment of company, science-oriented, research programs is elaborate testimony to the value placed on *scientific* creativity and the esteem in which it is held. Such centers do provide the company with technological improvements which may give them a temporary lead over their competition. And there is no doubt, too, that scientific research groups have been responsible for great progress benefiting the sponsoring company and its customers.

But, formal programs for fostering scientific creativity have seldom been paralleled by even the barest investigation of artistic creativity. While industry may recognize the advantages stemming from creative research and subsequent application of science, too often they ignore the tangible results which can accrue to them from the creative research and subsequent application of art. These tangible results can, on the whole, be achieved with far less cost. Elaborate science-type laboratories are not basic to requirements of artistic creativity.

It should be mentioned here that scientific creativity revolves around verifiable laws and systematized knowledge. Artistic creativity, on the other hand, without this familiar kind of measurement is often without obviously calculable results and, therefore, seems to be outside the successful routines of industry. Actually, it is this no-limit-to-the-imagination, no-planned-order, aspect of design that is its unassailable strength and attraction. It is the influence of this strength and attraction which industry so sorely needs.

The role of design in competitive identity

Walter Paepcke understood this need and the role which design could play in establishing identity and providing the competitive leverage for which he was searching. I would like to quote from a statement he made regarding the development of an advertising campaign.

"Under the circumstances, it was difficult to see how we could compete for the reader's attention. The pages of the publications which we had selected already were filled with the advertising of companies whose names had been household words for a generation or more. Our budget was a mere fraction of theirs and with it we were attempting to establish the same basic for public recognition and confidence it had taken them years to achieve.

"The more we thought about our predicament the more we came to realize that the idea in an advertisement is not always more important than the method of presentation. Even a commonplace idea, if left to itself and not confused with others, can be delivered with considerable impact when it is given graphic presentation that has taste. Design then becomes the instrument for giving an advertisement the esthetic and intellectual integrity that draws and holds attention. We reasoned that if we were to publish a series of advertisements in which modern design was the common denominator, in which copy on a single idea was limited to 15 words or less, we might have the formula that would serve our purpose. The reader would have something interesting to look at which he could associate with us; the originality, imagination and taste displayed would reflect similar qualities in our organization and our products."

Mr. Paepcke went on to say, "This was unorthodox advertising in its day and immediately became a subject of controversy. Among some businessmen and some professional advertising people it evoked a reaction bordering on shock, but those who praised it far outnumbered its detractors. And as the controversy continued, the visibilty and reader identification of the advertising increased out of all proportion to the dollars paid for it."

Mr. Paepcke *did not* demand measurement first. This was the key to the success of "Great Ideas" campaign. I recognize, however, that this attitude cannot normally be expected from most managements. He was the founder of the company and its head; thus he, like Adriano Olivetti, enjoyed prerogatives which many managements do not have. To satisfy most managements, some measurement is required before they will spend substantial money on a radical departure from the norm. This is particularly true when considering an expenditure for design.

To satisfy their requirement for measurement, and yet take advantage of the ingredient of design, management must be willing to depart from the norm — to experiment with new ideas for visual communication — and to sustain the efforts long enough for the impact to be of real value in separating them from their competitors.

Just as management makes use of scientific research programs, so must they also set up means for creative research in design and visual communications. Specifically, experimental campaigns should be developed and evaluated. These campaigns should not be based on prior judgments, surveys, and experiences. This would parallel, in design, the *carte blanche* freedom enjoyed by science in some of its relationships with management.

I want to stress the fact that these should be actual campaigns in order to realistically evaluate the contribution of design.

If managements take this action, they will have moved half way toward the utilization of the power of artistic creativity. Then it will be up to the design profession to meet business at the half way point — that point where the designers' efforts are clearly attuned to and contribute to management's goals.

With the establishment of the Bauhaus, designers recognized the relationship of their work to the machine age. Now designers must recognize the relationship of their work to the age of marketing. Now, as in the 1920's, design must accept the challenge, and understand the requirements of the business environment. The designer cannot intellectually remove himself from this environment and expect to reap the rewards provided by the business community.

The designer who does not work toward a better understanding between design and business, forgoes his great opportunity to utilize the economic power of business for raising our society's esthetic expression and appreciaiton.

COMMENTS BY MR. ECKERSTROM IN ANSWER TO QUESTIONS

Does Container Corporation have any yardstick, any measuring methods of the effectiveness of their visual communication?

We have measured the Great Ideas in several ways after the campaign was running, of course. We had a survey done about a year ago among purchasing agents, which is the group that we are basically trying to reach, purchasing agents of companies who buy our products.

They compared our advertising (and these were definite interviews) with that of our competition, and the results showed very strongly the effects of the Great Ideas campaign in their over-all attitude toward the company. Of particular interest was the fact that they did associate imagination and good design and creativity with the company, whereas they didn't with the others. That is a measurement.

We receive a considerable amount of mail every day regarding the ads and, of course, in any one year there has not been any more than 13 in one publication. So the fact that this mail continues each day is quite important to us.

I suppose half the high schools in the country use Great Ideas, and also I believe it is the only advertising currently being sold. We sell about 6,000 a year to people who write for them, without taking our company name off the ads.

What is your opinion of instruments in testing the visual efficiency of advertising and promotion methods?

Well, I think that there are many of these tests that have great value. When I suggested these experimental campaigns, I don't think this is all we have to do, but we certainly must take advantage of the testing resources that we have. Many of them are very, very good.

But we have to move beyond these testing devices. It is not like the scientific laboratory in this respect. I don't think we can find all the answers beforehand. I think this has been pretty well shown, and I think there are certain areas where testing is advisable, particularly those that have to be tried out in the field in the full scale operation and not in a test situation.

Since art is essentially an empirical approach and technology is a precise science, doesn't it often require a considerable period of time in experimenting to correlate and to arrive at a conclusion between a given approach in testing and the correllation of art and technology working out?

Yes. I think, certainly, that time is required — time and considerable money and effort.

I think that this is one of the things that is missing presently. There isn't enough time given to these things in this sense, and that's why an idea such as presented in relation to a specific campaign — that would have to run long enough to allow it to work, even after the time is spent for the research and the development of the campaign.

In this respect the design profession, in my opinion, has not done enough of its own research. This is another story — this and the whole problem of design education.

These areas are tied together and the design profession has never really united behind any kind of study of this kind, yet they do unite behind the shows and other expressions of this type, which I think are not nearly as fruitful and valuable as what these other things might do or reveal.

the television commercial: international communication medium

WILLIAM R. DUFFY
Senior Art Director, in charge of Television,
McCann-Erickson, Inc.

H. DONALD LAVINE
Creative Group Head, International Radio,
Television and Cinema,
McCann-Erickson, Inc.

SAMUEL MAGDOFF
Executive Producer,
Elektra Film Productions, Inc.

WILLIAM R. DUFFY: Shown on the next page are a few frames from an Italian commercial for Vick's Inhalers. The fact that the language spoken in the film is Italian is really unimportant. What is important is that almost anywhere in the world people would get the message. Change the sound track to French or Greek or Spanish or English and the humor, the selling approach, the consumer benefit would be just as valid. For this comes very close to being a universal commercial — one that is so basic in concept, in audience interest, in technique that it could do an effective selling job just about anywhere in the world.

Our subject, then, is really that of "universality" and we shall present it from the creative standpoint — writing, art direction and production.

Anyone active in television is especially aware of time — of the inflexibility of the allotted time segments and of the limitations this imposes. We know that if the subject, and its form of delivery, is of interest, there is never enough time. If it is boring — in either subject or delivery — even a second of time is more than enough.

Here, too, we must also be concerned with time. Our topic, the international market, is so broad that we will have to compress many of our thoughts and eliminate many areas we believe to be obvious, such as the business potentials, the creative challenges, and many technical problems.

H. DONALD LAVINE: It should be pointed out that, when we mention commercials here, we are referring to both TV and Cinema. It may come as a surprise to some that, outside of the United States, advertising in movie theatres is an extremely important medium, and has been for far longer than television. This is especially true in France where, as in other countries, there is still no *commercial* television. A second TV network is scheduled to start in France at the end of 1963, and it is thought that the cost of running it will be so high that, before long, advertising may be the only way to support it.

The primary differences between television and cinema are the use of color, the length, and the amount of entertainment as opposed to "sell." There is a philosophy which properly, we believe, contends that when an audience is paying money in a theatre to be entertained, the sell portion of the film must not be too overwhelming.

It should be emphasized, however, that not all commercials are universal in appeal or effectiveness. Far from it. There are still actually very few that fall into that category. Nevertheless, the day of the universal commercial is coming — and there are several good reasons for it.

Common market situations growing in Europe and other areas of the world, combined with improved transportation and communications between countries, have caused a greater interchange of ideas and cultures than ever before. Living standards are rising faster. Degrees of sophistication and understanding are beginning to level out. Traditional business procedures are more susceptible to change.

For example, until recently, the only French products one could buy in Germany were mostly agricultural products — without brand names. There were a few exceptions, of course, such as cognac, champagne and perfume. But today, there are many French products, with brand names, on German store shelves. And this situation is reciprocal.

As a result, international marketers in the area have had to solve the relatively new problem of product brand names. They are having to come up with names that can be spelled and pronounced properly in several different languages — names that do not carry unwanted meanings or connotations in the different countries and, in addition, names that can be registered as a trade-mark everywhere.

This is a difficult problem to solve, but one that shouldn't concern us too much here. The point is that it is being solved, and that brand-name products are crossing national borders to a greater extent than ever before. This will lead eventually to greater need for using one basic selling concept

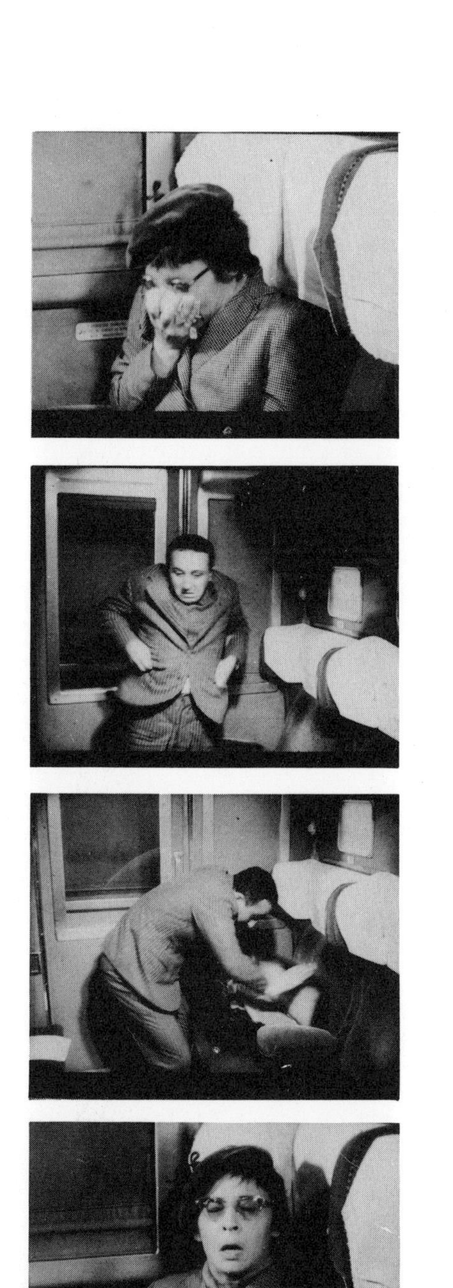
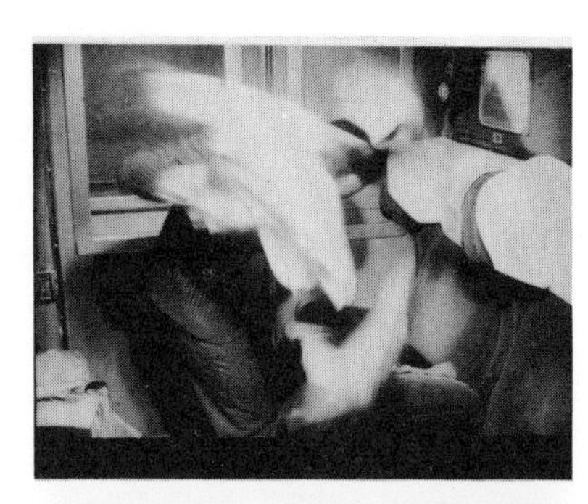
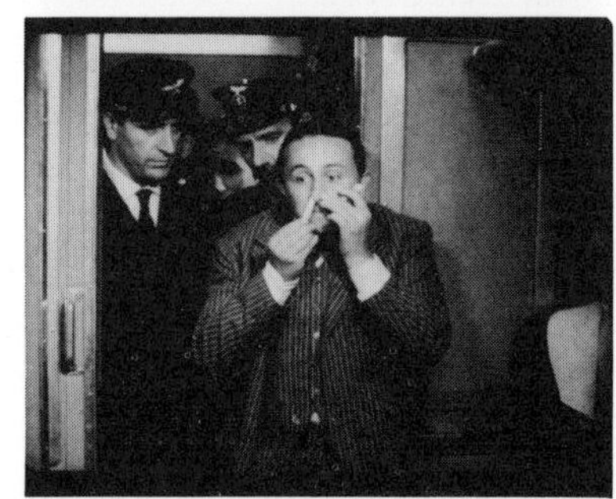

 for any given product in all countries, instead of the current confusion and waste inherent in the use of a different advertising campaign for each market.

Now, let us get something very clear. This does not mean forcing translated American commercials down the world's throat. We have a right to be proud of our many achievements in marketing and advertising. But we must not be blindly conceited. Experience has proved time and again that a good selling idea can come from anywhere and, with slight modifications, can be equally effective everywhere.

A film based on the typical boy-girl situation represents a universally accepted theme. For example, one was created and produced in Brazil. Then, translated from Portuguese to Spanish, it has since been adopted for a Kolynos Toothpaste campaign throughout Latin America. Though the music of this particular film was in the rhythm of the samba, there were originally other versions of it in everything from polkas to modern jazz.

That brings up another interesting area of universality. During a recent South American trip, I found that Paul Anka was every bit as popular with the teenagers in Buenos Aires as he is here. And the number one record in Brazil was Bat Masterson's TV show theme song in Portuguese!

In fact, acceptance of American music is becoming world-wide. Without knowing the actual percentages, I would guess that American-style music is the background for over 80 per cent of all Japanese TV commercials. Again, though, I must raise the caution that not everything American is perfect for other countries. If it is readily accepted, fine. But it cannot, and must not, be forced down their throats.

Several stills are shown here from a delightful commercial, created and produced in France, that demonstrate why the American solution to a problem is not necessarily the only, or even the best, solution. Compare the diagram, drawn by the mother to show the kids how Vick's Vaporub works, with the techniques we're currently using for pharmaceutical products in the United States. Perhaps we can learn something about casting, camera angles and, especially, demonstrations from this. That commercial shows, on the other hand, that France has learned something from us, too. Until recently, most European commercials — especially those of France and Italy — have suffered from what might be called "entertainment compulsion." The creators of these commercials were so busy entertaining that they would often forget to sell the product. In this respect, most current French and Italian commercials are beginning to show the influence of American selling "know-how." There has already been a great deal of this interchange of ideas and techniques.

From a 20-second Mexican commercial which demonstrates a universally accepted selling point: that, no matter how much of a hero you may be, the girls still go for the man who is well groomed. The approach here is basic, though highly exaggerated.

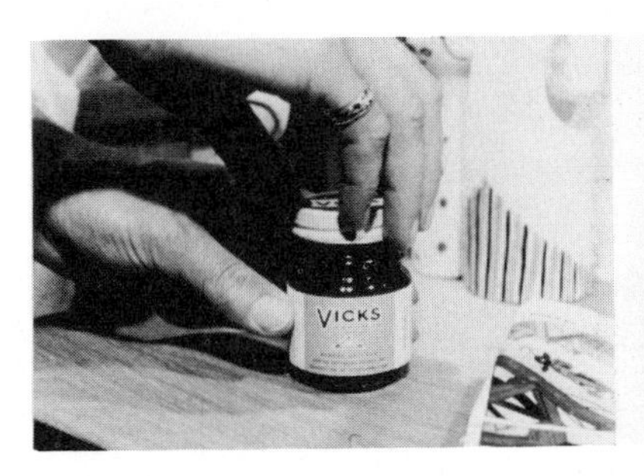

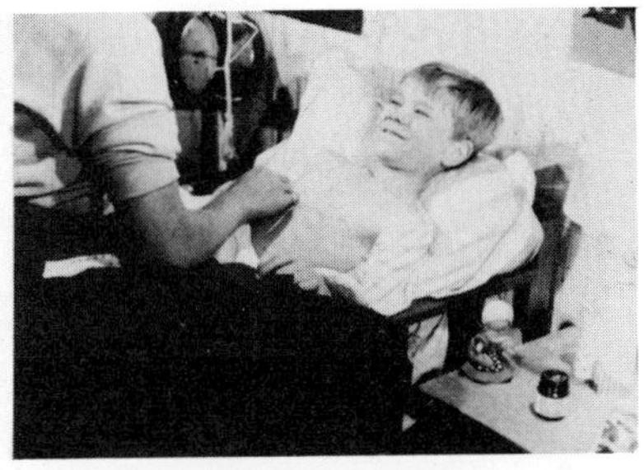

It is, in fact, only through greater interchange of such ideas and techniques that truly good international selling concepts can be discovered and utilized fully. We have much to learn from each other, in other words.

Humor is another example of the growing universality. In recent years, we have become familiar with a fresh, new, off-beat type of humor which we tend to think of as being strictly American in its sophisticated appeal. It might surprise you, therefore, to discover that a film, produced in Australia for Nestle's Sunshine Powdered Milk, was voted the most popular commercial of the year. (Two frames are illustrated here.)

SAMUEL MAGDOFF: Shown here are stills from two commercials that are excellent examples of a film technique called "stop motion." They have as their basic concept the building of mood or emotion toward the image of the products and their use. The first was produced in Spain for Tio Pepe Brandy. The second was produced in Argentina for Pera Grau Brandy. Other than both being brandy commercials, they bear a certain resemblance to each other.

Actually, of course, these two commercials are practically identical as to concept, music, movement and so forth. The differences are only in the names of the products and a few of the backgrounds. Here is the way this kind of thing happens. Through an organization known as ISAS, it is often possible to buy the rights to a cinema commercial for use in another country if there is no conflict of products in the market. In this case, the Argentine company bought the rights from the Spanish company. Then, they just duplicated it shot for shot, using the local product instead.

As was said before, a good selling idea can come from anywhere; it can be effective anywhere. Interchange of these ideas is the key. And this interchange is taking place at an ever-increasing rate. The advent of the Telstar communication satellite in July 1962 should give it a still greater boost. Countries around the world are currently planning and building receiving stations that will pick up the signals being bounced off of it. And though Telstar is still in the experimental stage — with its transmission period severely limited in time — it is certainly the forerunner of one of the most exciting developments of the television medium: intercontinental TV.

Another major factor in the growth of this interchange is the number of international film festivals being held each year. Some of the more important ones — like those at Venice, Cannes, Mar Del Plata in Argentina, Rio and Hollywood — attract world-wide attention, and get entries from just about every country that boasts a film industry. As a result, each country's production and creative people are being exposed to not only the cultures of other countries, but to their latest developments in production, as well.

Another factor in the interchange of production techniques is the interchange of production personnel. Never before has there been so much international moving-around of cameramen and technicians. This has resulted in a great "learning-from-each-other" program that is far more significant than even the people in the film industry may realize.

For example, two Frenchmen opened a production company in Rio de Janeiro a year or two ago, and are fast becoming the busiest animation house there. Because of their influence, one begins to find a slightly French design quality in much of the current Brazilian animation. The Spanish film companies are showing the influence of the Russian school of film-making, due to Russian training of Spanish technicians. Certain Dutch technicians, now in Italy, are influencing Italian stop-motion films. And we, in the United States, are using many French and Italian cameramen and German special effects technicians.

European production has rubbed off on us in other ways, too. Imagine an American automobile manufacturer of even five years ago daring *not* to show his product until almost the very end of the commercial! Yet, this idea

of selling by mood, emotion and excitement — which was an accepted form of advertising approach outside the United States for many years — is now a recognized technique here today.

WILLIAM R. DUFFY: In the past, nations — their peoples, their prevailing characteristics, their representative films — have been rather rigidly "typed" and "over-generalized."

For example, we have come to recognize Italian films for their sincere, warm, candid qualities, for their natural casting and for the "earthiness" of their basic content.

In French films, we have come to expect that the content will be sophisticated, with a lavish, fashion approach to both casting and production plus the finesse of fine acting and execution.

However, films from Germany and Holland have represented the opposite character, with little emotion or warmth while excelling in the qualities of their technical and design precision and even perfection.

Today, however, we can see a change in the traditional attitudes and beliefs. This change is due to the cross-pollination of thinking, to greater exposure, to greater interest in what others are doing, and to the way others are living and working. This is a healthy interest, a profitable interchange. The results of all this, though still in the formulative stage, resemble the interplay existing in the print graphics where the entire world has learned from and followed much of the exploration and teachings of the German, French and Swiss design pioneers.

Today, there is a greater awareness and interest in what other nations are doing in the area of communication through the television and motion picture media. These media have become, in fact, a major method of entertainment, education and selling the world over. The general interest is pointed up by the work of organizations such as the Canadian Film Board and the array of annual international film festivals, and by the recognition given by both industry and government in the United States.

An example of the values of this interchange is a cosmetic commercial from Germany, illustrated here by several frames. It represents a definite departure from the usual stark and cold Germany treatment, reflecting the warmth of French and Italian methods of casting along with some slight, but definite, American influences. Here, a traditional element of German films — precision — has been retained and blended with the elements borrowed from other countries. There is the warmth of the action portion of the picture, precisely matted within the cold outlines of a compact. This is by no means a great commercial, but it does represent significant stages in the striving for universality and the interchange of ideas.

It is a common belief among Americans in general, and much of Madison Avenue in particular, that sophistication ends abruptly north of Westport and west of Short Hills. In reality, the audiences of the world are exposed on an everyday basis to films and commercials that run here only in our so-called "art houses."

This Spanish commercial for G.P. Tea shows something of the international acceptance and understanding of modern, decorative, sophisticated design treatments in animation — American-style animation — plus the simplicity of story line and the uses of symbolism which have become a major factor in all areas of visual communication.

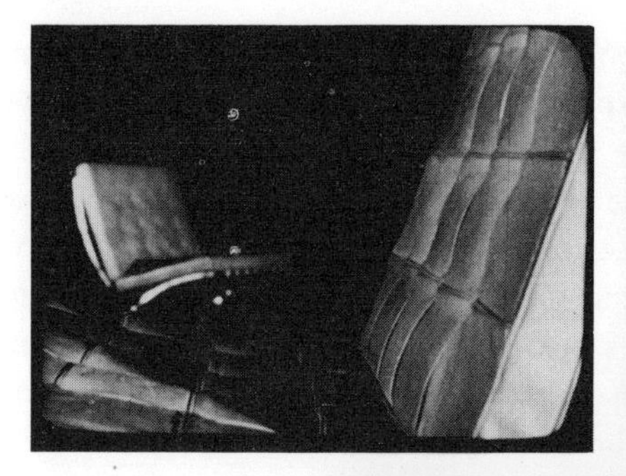
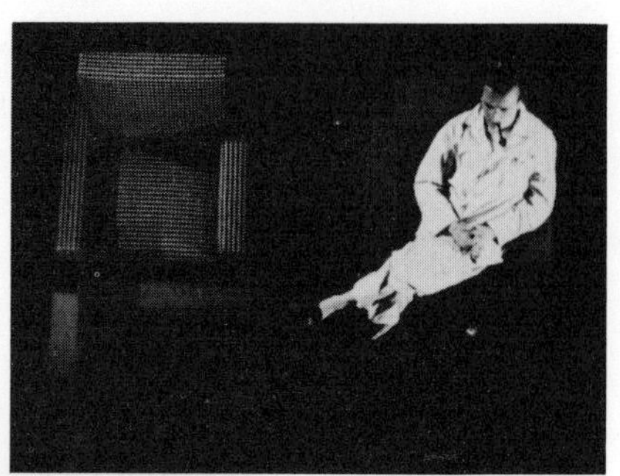
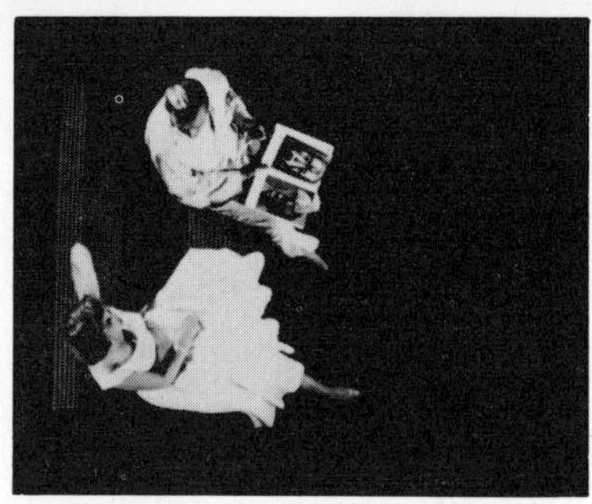

Significant from an image-building standpoint in the display and artistic demonstration of the product, its manufacture and usage is the example shown here (three frames only). It has impact, attention-getting-and-holding interest, as well as a long-lived potential. The film is from Spain, a commercial for Knoll International, and is designed for extended usage.

Pioneers in television have been concerned with many of the same problems in domestic communication that are now arising in the international field. We are all familiar with the concern of the late Harold Ross of *The New Yorker* for that "little old lady in Dubuque," and with the fact that the people in the advertising business picked it up and were too often heard to say: "Sure, that's great for New York, but will they understand it in Dubuque?" Most of us have long since learned that they do. Now, in fact, today's question might be: "Never mind about Dubuque, will they understand it is Istanbul — and buy it in Bombay?" *We think they will!*

All of the commercials, of which just a few of their stills or frames can be reproduced here, could be shown anywhere, with only slight modifications, and still communicate their intended messages. None of these films is really localized in basic appeal, or design, or understanding, because each represents a strong common denominator — an international language — the language of vision. This language, this method of communication, is becoming, like music, one of the major communication techniques in an international market.

Universal not only in the language of vision but of sound, by employing an audio device (the distinctive sound of a motor scooter), this Italian commercial for Vespa created a unique "property" for the product. An almost perfect example of universality, it conveys the spirit and image of the product and of those who use it. This film has no dialogue at all, yet the viewer is left with a "sound" impression.

chic by design: the communication of fashion

OLEG CASSINI
Dress Designer

A wise man once said: "The true art of attiring women must be based on concepts of simple beauty and modest originality. It must enhance her outward presentation and re-affirm her virtue, her stature, her sovereign position, in a world that's run by men — harried men who long to be surrounded by beautiful, enticing women. To that it is important to add today that it must, perforce, allow every passerby to realize that she is a woman." This is a quotation from a Roman philosopher of 23 centuries ago.

Much have we changed our mores and living conditions since then, much have we improved our arts and sciences. But, frankly, we must acknowledge the undeniable truth that we cannot add a modest wrinkle to the above considerations concerning the clothing for our charming ladies.

The definition of the word "chic," in the second edition of Webster's Unabridged Dictionary, stresses "elegance" and "originality."

So, we're exactly back where the discerning Roman was — 23 centuries ago. True, we're no longer on the Via Appia, but on 7th Avenue, where numerous leaders and would-be leaders in the exciting field of making money by designing and manufacturing dresses are attempting to interest or invent the essential concepts that were already established three centuries before B.C. became A.D.

Since these attempts are basically futile, the true conception of art is unwarily being drowned in a choppy and treacherous sea of intrigue, pettiness, doubtful taste and navigable amounts of dubious double-talk.

Who, then, is the enemy of American couture? That nervous little man who starts his irksome day with such a hangover that he has to have a drink before breakfast — a cocktail made up of equal parts of propinquity, absurdity, social enmity, mediocrity and anonimity. It's shaken in cracked ice, and the effect impedes his taking advantage of the handsomeness of our American woman. The edgy little man is shortsighted. His design for clients is anything but constructive. It fills closets with styles that generally destroy the lovely image of our beautiful ladies.

Military tailors can make battalions of men look chic — and look identical, which is proper for bellicose regimentation. But, alas, we don't want our women to undergo such a leveling treatment. Much too precious are women to be strapped down by crippling styles that ignore the anatomy and the poetry that conform the body of a woman.

Dress is one of the most outstanding means of distinction for a person — and etymology explains that a "person" is a being able to produce its own sound. Ladies must be dressed as persons — in the etymological sense.

Madame De Sevigne — perhaps apocryphally — is supposed to have said: "To be in love is like being well dressed." The best dressed lady in the Louvre Museum is one whose head and arms were amputated by the winds of time. She is only dress, a flowing dress of such lightness that it defies its being wrought of marble — the Winged Victory of Samothrace.

Although I do not wish to infer that I admire the Greta Garbo look, or the Madame Pandit look, or the Queen Elizabeth look, I do bless their designers for making them look — individually — like Greta Garbo, like Madame Pandit, like Queen Elizabeth. I should be most chagrined if the self-appointed czars of 7th Avenue were to succeed in dressing *all* these colorful ladies in the same unimaginative uniform!

In this land of free enterprise — barring a few freakish exceptions — success and recognition, in our unpredictable field of design, will eventually come to those who best create and work, to those who enhance the beauty that nature has graciously planted in our vicinity of place and time. Such must be the role of the enlightened designer, for this makes him the paladin in the art of giving freedom and, thence, beauty to his task. Similarly, I foresee fantastic progress in styles — because of the advent of textiles that do not fade, or wrinkle, or stain or rip as the lady sits on the hirsute back of her medieval horse. Gone are the days of the velours of Byzantium, which could not be washed, and which were worn over corsets ribbed with pieces of steel or whalebone, and whose cruel and painful aim is now being properly replaced by skimmed milk, Metrecal and rounds of golf.

Functionalism and technocracy have given us freedom of design in architecture. We no longer need, for instance, the girding buttress for the lofty Gothic cathedral. Our steel structures now enable us to construct slim buildings, 100 stories high, wherein the titanic strength is but a subtle element hidden by graceful structural agility. We no longer need to have respect or tolerance for pretentious demagogues whose dogmas are now easily destroyed. In our present civilization, we believe in legitimate proofs and tangible results, which are the only important product of man's efforts.

I do not concede that, in order to create styles for women, masculinity — on the part of the designer — must be decapitated. In a field akin, that of painting, men have been the best and most immortal renderers of the beauty of women. Virility does for a normal appreciation of the lady's loveliness. This truism goes back to the days when a troglodytic girl's Sunday best consisted of an unlined piece of leopard skin.

" 'Tis as right as rain
in the plain
in China — or in Spain."

I am appalled by the incredible fact that the so-called judges of "The Best Dressed Women in the World" have seldom laid eyes on them. 'Twould seem to be only natural that the opinion of an elegance-contest judge be based on his having seen the best dressed ladies. In the case of a lady of prominence, this exigency is somewhat lessened, for the public sees her often, in newspaper or magazine photographs, or on TV or newsreels. The elegance of such ladies is subject to constant public scrutiny. This phenomenon is a good sword with two reciprocating edges. The British public is conscious of Princess Margaret's meticulous dress and she is conscious that she is being watched by all, not only by her private photographer. This is a wholesome situation, and no myths can be woven about the actual appearance of such a lady of international prominence. Therefore, it becomes her inevitable responsibility to use discriminating taste, to seek the cooperation of cognizant and inspired artists. This, again, is the result of the interplay that governs our social and industrial freedom. Let us keep it alive and unfettered! It is due to the exercise of such precious freedom of private decision that my associates and I are proud to see that our heartfelt dedication to our art has met with generous and honoring success, and has — if you'll pardon our normal lack of modesty — so much strengthened the once fragile trappings of the nascent American Couture, which is now a universally acknowledged and admired industry of our country. The products of this new American industry are worn today by elegant and satisfied ladies in practically every country in the world.

The elegant lady from Dallas, San Francisco or Cape Canaveral may go to Paris to buy her trousseau; or she may buy domestic copies of European couture, which copies are sometimes well made, sometimes atrocious. But, when she decides to buy American, she can now find beautiful, functional clothes that are correctly designed for the woman who leads the American form of life.

A bard of the 18th century — when women had the strength on which some kings based a goodly part of their power — said:

Let us have ladies who have strength, as such
Women whose grace one cannot touch
For it is made of poetry divine
As tenuous and as subtle as the stringest vine.

If I may be allowed a brief indulgence in ego, I shall tell you that I was born in the heady Europe of the First World War — where the privilege of being properly and elegantly dressed was reserved, exclusively, for the wealthy and powerful. Fashion of taste and quality, such as it was in those days, was costly and extremely scant. The masses that did away with the French kings and (later) with the Russian czars were ill-fed, trodden upon and very badly clothed. In my new American country, the millions of voters who caused the latest democratic change of government were abundantly fed, free and quite well dressed. This is progress!

Against our enemies, we may be temporarily winning some battles and losing some battles, but one battle we are winning every day is that of styles in attire. This point, which may seem unimportant to many citizens, is actually quite meaningful. For it is undeniable that the most oppressing dictators and despots of all the ages have seldom sought to impose or succeeded in imposing, their mandates regarding the dress of the people. The concept of the style of dress has swayed, changed and developed with the free tide of public opinion and of the prevailing social requirements through the centuries — as political conquests have punctuated the pages of history from the Egyptians to the Assyrians, Persians and Hebrews, from the Greeks to the Romans, from the Byzantines to the Saracens and Moors, throughout Medieval Europe and the eternal Orient; from the Conquistadors of Spain to the Emperors of Britain and the Louis of France; from the American young men who went West, to those who made the 'twenties roar, to those who pose as beatniks and those who twist at the Peppermint Lounge. Always has the style of dress been a matter of individual taste and choice.

Therefore, it is our duty to work with a sense of responsibility that stems from a source of deep historical momentum. Let us not counter the dictums of society and its assets and limitations as we develop style. We must make the most and the best that we can with the very advanced developments of materials and the liberality of taste that we now enjoy in this country. Thus did the realm surge and die for the Nilotic postiches, the Phrygian bonnets, the Tyrian veils, the Cypriote girdles, the Napoleonic falsies, the Zori and the Gheta of the Japanese, the Georgian breeches, the Spanish mantillas and the dirty sneakers of Greenwich Village. Evolution is riding the crest of all its highest waves. Thus, the current style of Americans of good taste must continue developing and going forth into the wide, wide world of fashion.

Who's winning the Cold War of Fashion? The answer is quite evident. Over scores of years, we've seen no American Presidents or their wives copy the attire of the Chinese or the Russians. I rather believe that all the people in the world are gradually adopting the trends of style that we are developing in the United States of America. This leadership of ours imposes the corresponding responsibilities on our design and manufacturing ateliers. This is not a small responsibility. We must work with inspiration, devotion and integrity, with taste and functionalism. And perhaps we must begin by annihilating the spurious trade publications that becloud the basic issues of fashion and act under the sick impulse of jealousy and ignorance — all in the name of "Volume" — because, as mentioned above, this is a field that breeds only in absolute freedom, the freedom to chose intelligently that which is most becoming and adequate for the individual.

When I ponder over the responsibility that is ours, as artists, I realize we have an obligation to continue making available, to the American and foreign ladies, products that will prove, in history, that our society launched materials, techniques and styles that evidence our extraordinary age — an age in which a German violin player settled in our United States and broke the atom.

to the picture-minded, who is really communicating?

a panel discussion

CHARLES T. COINER
Moderator
Vice President, Executive Art Director,
N. W. Ayer & Son, Inc.

AUSTIN BRIGGS
Illustrator

ART KANE
Photographer

HENRY KOERNER
Painter

GEORGE McNEIL
Painter,
Professor of Art History, Pratt Institute

MR. COINER:

Communication, I think we will all agree, is a rather over-worked word nowadays. We hear it used extensively in the technical field. In fact, I was told recently that there is more communication over the wires between machines, from one machine to another, than there is between people. However, we are interested here primarily in communication between people.

To define this more closely, what we are interested in is communication by means of pictures, between people and not by machines. This rather narrows it down, but considering how the use of pictures has expanded in recent years, we have an area large enough to cover in the space allotted here.

Our public is picture-minded and whether we, as experts, like it or not, the public is becoming sophisticated — in the pictures they choose to live with, the pictures they get their information from and the pictures they are enertained by.

There has been considerable research on this subject on the part of advertising agencies and publications, but there is still much we do not know. What does a painter communicate to an office worker who comes into a gallery and buys an abstract painting on the installment plan? What is it that the painter is communicating to that person to cause him to give up hard-earned money for a little picture to put in his home, to study and to derive pleasure from?

In contrast to the wider use of pictures throughout our country in all forms of communication, why is it that the illustrator is having such a hard time these days? I know of a very prominent illustrator of a few years ago whose sole occupation right now is walking his wire-haired terrier in the park. What is happening? Is illustration dead?

Films are being used for such varied purposes and in so many different places, including the permanent collections of art museums. The Metropolitan Museum, for example, says that it now intends to look broadly at the proposition that photography is an art. Yet *Time* magazine, which is certainly knowledgeable on communications, will use an artist to paint a portrait for its cover, whenever its schedule allows. One of those painters is on our panel — Henry Koerner.

These and many other questions come to mind, for discussion by this panel, and perhaps we can come up with a few answers. Each panelist will cover the broad area of his specialty, rather than only his particular work. So, with this general introduction, let us begin.

AUSTIN BRIGGS:

Living in France, as I have been doing for some months, has been an interesting problem. For, living in the middle of a revolution, as it were, I have been able to gain some perspective on the revolution in American graphic communication.

I believe that I am as productive a part of American illustration as I have been for many years. I did not go to France to retire and, in that strange phrase, "paint." I manage to make a good many, to me, satisfying observations in my commercial work. My pride in my profession is a fierce one, even when the profession is in bad health. I have never failed to remember that the prestige and welfare of the people I work for is inseparable from my own, and that my best hope for an audience lies in an affiliation with "the establishment," even though I cannot always join it.

In France, I found an opportunity to look at advertising and publishing in America from a greater distance than Connecticut. I find them changed, but not unrecognizable. The cafés in my "quarter" look like ant-hills inadvertently kicked over, out of which streams every type and tongue and color — including *café au lait*. The Sorbonne is a block away, and the students are as inquisitive and acquisitive as those on Madison Avenue — and sometimes just as difficult to understand.

I have reached some small conclusions. If the artist is, first of all, an "eye," I believe that some of the eyes working today are opaque. The representations of bits of string and cardboard boxes we have seen in recent graphic efforts evoke predictable feelings — feelings about boxes and string! They are clichés, just as thoroughly as the clichés they are meant to replace, and bear little resemblance to a human message to which we can easily relate.

To me, form and content belong in the same embrace, and the public we address is living today in the form of today. It is ironic to perceive in some of the "new" illustration, the using and re-using of old material, the sensibilities and points of departure which were part of Vuilliard's repertoire in France in 1900. Ronald Firbank once remarked that, "What is new is frequently only that which we have forgotten." There is a difference between the truly dramatic and the seeking for theatrical effects! What is most striking among the "new" work is the extreme mannerism — and *so* much alike. I should think a certain prejudice towards one's own point of view would be helpful. The "manner" is good, but I am certain that it will prove unmanageable as the "new" illustrator faces the inevitable "new" problems, and he will be trapped in his style like a boxer who can only move to his left.

I feel no hostility to the photograph as an art form. Art is created by the man, not by the tool. But find irony, too, in the photographers' attitude that they are the "elite" of illustration. Many of them have no doubts and are assisted in this belief by the fact that all but a very few illustrators have abdicated. One speaker at last year's Illustrators Society seminar advocated making paintings and drawings *more* photographic in order to gain *wider* acceptance! Should those of us who draw forget that the artist-photographer is, unlike ourselves, at the mercy of a dumb instrument? Should we forget that the "moment of truth" may equally be a "moment of lies"? I believe many of us have forgotten that in the end nothing is believable but truth itself. We may also have forgotten that truth, in the graphic sense, lies in the field of the specific. I am most disturbed by the disappearance of the "object." In art it is the "object" that truly counts, not the "subject."

I own a Calder and a Henry Moore and the walls of my house carry many abstract paintings. But, as I said, the public desires a message to which it can easily relate, and much abstract art appears to echo the protest of one of the "beat" poets at the "indignity of being understood."

Sketched on Board
—Sailing into
Curaçao

In our efforts to communicate with the masses — to create the most attractive ambiance for our message — we have forgotten that ambiance is the sum of certain facts. The temperature, the color, the smell, or perhaps an act — the total of these assembled specifics. We have neglected to remember that the mass is composed of individuals who are interested primarily in the particular. To state the situation in another way: We seem to have been thinking that the masses require a general truth because we have considered the mass to be general in nature, failing to appreciate that the mass — like us — only apprehends that experience which is generally true when it is presented in the particular. Our senses are barely able to recognize the specific out of a world full of impossible-to-choose-from generalities. It is the visual communicator's job to make those choices which can deliver the desired message — *the one specific statement which is uniquely not general but is, nevertheless, absolutely familiar.*

I must make certain that my meaning is not misunderstood. Realism, to me, means graphic truth, but I do not suggest that we, like Christopher Isherwood, become cameras with the shutter left open. On the contrary, I believe in distortion for the sake of clarity, balance and design. Visual communication starts with a concept organized in terms of visual fact, which is then delivered to the public in a form surrounded by such allusions and insights as will dramatize its meaning and compel the public to understand it more fully. It must be a precise representation of logical relationships.

I can give you a word example: I looked out my window at the trees in the Place de l'Estrapade and thought, "The trees are in flower with birds." (Do you see what I mean?)

In conclusion — and as another example — I'll tell you a story of an experience my wife had in Paris. We were returning home with a visiting friend after a late dinner and passed an entertainingly low night club which doesn't specialize in wives. It's called "The Cat Which Fishes." My friend and I decided to watch the fishing, my wife to go home to bed. My wife told me later that the cab driver questioned her on the way home. He couldn't believe that a wife would willingly allow her husband to go off to such a place. When he was convinced that I was her husband he praised her all the rest of the journey for being such an understanding woman.

Arriving at our front door he reached around, my wife thought, to shake hands. Instead he clutched her left bosom and gazed soulfully into her eyes. Her first impulse was to scream bloody murder, but my wife had lived in Paris long enough. She said calmly, "Monsieur, I am the woman of my husband!" Instantly the driver let go, leaped from his cab, ran around and opened the door. He followed my wife to our *porte* where he picked up the hem of her coat and kissed it, murmuring "Madame, you are a Queen!" As he walked back to his taxi he turned and waved, "*à bientôt.*" My wife replied, "*à bientôt.*"

That's communication!

ART KANE:

I'd like to begin with a quote from Cole Porter who said "Birds do it, Bees do it, Even educated fleas do it." He was, of course, referring to falling in love. If, by chance, the subject were changed to the making of a photograph the lyric might come out something like: "I do it, You do it, So can monkeys in the zoo do it."

For there's no question that a cable release extended from the shutter of a Rollei to the paw of a slightly curious monkey would result in a perfectly credible picture. My five-year-old son can set off the mechanism for taking a picture. I'm not bragging. So can anybody else's. So can a dog or a cat or perhaps an apple falling from a tree set off the mechanism for taking a picture.

Anyone or anything can take a picture. Family albums are loaded with pedestrian but nonetheless concrete evidence of this fact. The Eiffel Tower, the Trevi Fountain, the Grand Canyon, the Casbah, the Pyramids, and all the other landmarks of the world are constantly surrounded by hundreds of faceless creatures who hide behind one-eyed masks and who choose to see the world as a series of unrelated rectangular images.

About two or three years ago *Life* magazine reported on the Camera Craze. The statistics on how many people are taking pictures and how much photographic equipment is being sold is staggering. (This story was told with words and *pictures.*) I can remember going to the Bronx Zoo when I was a kid and envying the other kids that sported baby Brownies around their necks. Today this same zoo or any other zoo is the hunting ground for kids whose Hasselblads and 400 mm. lenses are giving them curvatures of the spine. Therefore, we must assume and accept the fact that a mature and creative human being is not a necessary factor in the mere taking or execution of a photographic image. We must accept the fact that it is even possible for the camera to take its own picture by accidentally falling in such a manner as to trigger its own shutter release. We must also accept the fact that, whether it be man, animal, fruit, vegetable or the force of gravity that sets the machine in action, either one can occasionally result in an inspired picture. I have known many amateurs who have occasionally taken brilliant photographs. The Metropolitan Museum has seen fit to display some in recent exhibitions as works of art.

This all speaks well for photography as a medium but does not speak well for photographers as individuals.

In defense of photographers devoting their lives to their craft, I can justly say that in this mechanized art form one can only judge ability and creativity through a large body of one's work or through the sum total of an individual's work and never by the result of a dabble. Nevertheless, these dabbles have to be contended with and must also be respected. If produced accidentally, we need not respect the executor but we must respect the result.

Can a photographer simultaneously be a doctor, lawyer or Indian chief? No, but every doctor, lawyer, Indian chief, bank robber and 5th grader can practice photography. Moreover, because the materials used and because the end result, chemically and physically if not esthetically, is identical to that of the professional, these honest, well meaning individuals regard their work with modest esteem.

A short time ago I made a statement in a photography magazine to the effect that I hate cameras — and I do. Cameras are machines and are therefore not creative. The human mind can be creative and yet I sense a deterioration of this function as brought on by the Industrial Revolution and the machine men it has produced. A man who communicates through a machine must supersede the machine, must overpower it. Machines are tolerable only when they respond to man's desires and impulses, only when they are the slaves and we are the masters — they otherwise breed repetition, monotony and destruction. Before photography, pictures were created by people, not machines. It took years of intensive training to produce a picture maker, and only those chosen few were able to put inspired images on paper or canvas. Their medium was theirs alone, and the lay public looked on with respect and admiration. In those times it took a lot of training and a certain degree of talent to even produce a *bad* or mediocre maker of pictures. Today it takes about $3.00 and the amount of time necessary to remove the Brownie from the plastic bag.

Not only are there too many photographers but, consequently, there are too many pictures. And these pictures are somehow distorting our senses. They are taking all the wonder and mystery out of real life. They're supplying us with all the assumed answers and producing, on the one hand, a society of complacent individuals who remain satisfied with vicarious rather than actual experience and, on the other hand, with a society of energetic

and romantic individuals whose actual experience never lives up to the great illusion of the imaginary world experienced on the printed page.

The one group doesn't exert much effort. Why go to the South Pacific? There's always *Holiday* magazine. Why make love? There's always a Brigette Bardot movie. The other group makes the effort. They go to the South Pacific but find it disappointing because of the influence of the preconceived image already established by the pictures they saw. Or they try to emulate the screen lover and find that it doesn't work out the same way with the rollers in the wife's hair and without the Dmitri Tiomkin background music.

Where do we find these pictures? In magazines, newspapers, books, movie theaters, on billboards, television, railroad terminals, cereal boxes, subways, buses, taxicabs, sandwich men, restaurant place mats, post cards and match books, to name a few. From the moment you wake up in the morning and light your first cigarette to the time at night when you turn off the late, late show, you're constantly and unwillingly subjected to this greatest of all intruders — the picture.

We smoke because ever since childhood we've been brainwashed by pictures into believing that we're incomplete without a cigarette. That the symbol of real maturity and success is a cigarette. That you can't get a girl without a cigarette. Women by the thousands are buying some silly smelling perfume called Tabu in vain hope that one day they'll be attacked by some nut with a violin.

Now, I'm not saying all this to be nasty or to be funny either. If I were addressing a group of amateur photographers at the local Camera Club, I'm sure many people would be offended (and rightly so) but to no avail. Nothing would be gained.

But in addressing the inner core, the practicing photographer or those concerned with the medium as an esthetic means of visual communication, I feel somewhat justified in displaying these reactions and in criticizing a lot of well-meaning, harmless citizens. For it is not really these citizens whom I condemn, but the working photographer who, in the face of all this unending mediocrity and visual hypocrisy, does all too little to recognize it, consider it, evaluate it and above all, fight it in the only way he can and should — by making pictures, not taking pictures. Fighting the camera because of its availability to the millions of lay people all over the world. Fighting it because this same camera in their hands produces an abundance of mediocrity. Fighting it because this same camera in their hands produces an occasional work of art.

67 A working photographer must realize that it's a lot tougher to be an individual in this medium than almost any other and that he's contributing to a field already overloaded with pictures. With that in mind, he must never be satisfied with himself because his art is partially dependent on a machine and this machine performs indiscriminately for whoever picks it up.

HENRY KOERNER:

Everything and everybody is communicating. But it is also obvious that there is a hierarchy of communication. That means that certain communications are very deep, they are all-embracing, they are unforgettable, they are forever.

The great question is: Does this communication, if it is that deep, change human nature? Nobody is ever going to answer this. The only thing is that if it does not change, at least it makes our state of being possible.

Stripped of all his garments the great Houdini stands ready to enter another combination of confinements. The steel cases, all the locks, and every part of his body have been carefully searched for concealed tools. He shakes hands with the officers, with the examining doctors who wish him well and finally with his own assistant. He climbs into his imprisonments and the locks are thrown. Then, Houdini accomplishes the incredible — he manages to escape again! He has done this with what is called the world over "the Fake," slipped to him in that last unsuspected handshake.

God hovered the universe, all angels under his garment. He said goodbye to naked Adam, leaving him behind on his prison, earth. But in that last touch of hands, God gave Adam "the Fake" by which man can escape his tragedy — his tragedy which is not his crimes nor punishments, nor death, but his not knowing.

Instead of the apple from the tree of knowledge, God had given man for his escape key, "Art." It was only through art creativity that man could again and again escape his prison to be once more with his "Ba-al G'vuros," the master of all strength and all power.

Art, in this sense, is the basis of all religion, giving communication with the living God. In its greatest statement art does not illustrate religion, it *is* religion.

When I was a schoolboy in beautiful Vienna I spent many afternoons in the amusement park of the Prater. This place was hypnotic for me as, later on, was Marble Arch in London with its multitudes of speakers and hecklers, and Coney Island, New York's Sodom by the Sea.

In the Prater, barkers of the sideshows promised miracles to me, stage

"The Parade" — Courtesy Whitney Museum of American Art

performances by fakirs, fortune tellers, and fakes. There was the lure of the torture chamber and, greatest of all, the circus act with its major attraction, the human cannonball.

At Easter time, Vienna's church bells flew to Rome and, finally, Christ was resurrected. Amid thousands, I gazed at the "Savior" carried three times around the block. Of course, by 1939 all of greater Germany had become one huge torture chamber. And then, later, the human cannonball developed into today's spaceman.

The great spectacles — the Coliseums, Circuses, Shrines, and Launching Pads — are always with us and within us. In the inescapable arena of life each man still goes through his heroic act of living. He still transforms and resets his pattern of being, always with the greatest ingenuity.

Who, then, are the persecuted and the persecutors? The ruled and the rulers? The innocent and the depraved? The famous and the infamous? Who are the lovers and the loved? What is the position of God and man?

What is the position of God and man? This is our eternal question and eternal quest. As I said, religion arose and remains today as the artistic history of man's search for the image of God. We seek for His graven image, the subject matter, the episodes, and the motives that might reveal the mystery of our Maker.

By means of the image — the image, not the maker — and great art, man has praised both the living God and his own being, attempting in the process to free himself from his own tragedy, which is his Not Knowing.

It has not mattered if the celebration or communication has been with deeds, or incised in stone, or fashioned with music, paint, black line, or with words. A Moses, a Heracles, a Giotto, Goethe, Breughel, Beethoven, Melville, or a Cezanne have accomplished their acts of transformation, their acts of resetting the life pattern, with the greatest ingenuity possible for them.

Their achievements are our inspiration and challenge. Their records in communicating are our measures.

GEORGE MCNEIL:

There is a certain logic in my being placed last in this section, because the kind of art which I will present has entered the world of art recently, namely: "Abstract Expressionism."

Sometimes I wonder if this art is the last step in the pictorial representation which began with the Renaissance or whether it is the first part of a true revolution. But no matter how you consider its place, I think you will agree that any discussion of communication calls for a particular definition of this highly abstract art in its relation to communication.

Those who are engaged in the visual communication of ideas are involved in an instrumental art, just as practically all of the art made since Giotto. You start out with a certain purpose, and then by pictorial means you try to communicate certain ideas. You try to make these ideas more effective by bringing in the matter of feeling, and to the extent that you can make a sensuous ideological communication, you are that much more effective.

Now, sometime — maybe a hundred years ago, roughly 1850 or 1860 — there really was a great change in the nature of art, where the ideas that formerly were all-important — in a word, the story — began to become less and less important, and the means by which these ideas were being communicated — the line, the light and dark, the color, the texture, and all these other means which are made to create form — began to become increasingly important.

One might say that previously what had been a means to an end, the organization of color and form, now increasingly became the end of art and that the story, so-called, became less and less important.

One might say that in this transition from story or idea to abstraction there is a new subject, and that is the subject of the artist. If you think of a revolution in terms of development, where the revolution is a kind of climatic circumstance which makes prior beginnings somehow dramatic and exciting, then we can say that, for example, when Picasso made his first abstractions they simply made real and tangible what had been a long process (over 50 or 60 years) of prior development. The idea became more and more subordinated.

Now then, consider instrumentality. What was Monet interested in conveying when he made his pictures of the populace, or Renoir of those children? There wasn't any message, but rather a hope of giving a visual delight.

We then come to abstraction, per se. It is simply a furthering of this same intent. Where pictures are not about things, they are about themselves. And where art is not concerned with somehow dealing with means, it must exist as its own end.

If it is said that abstraction is something new, then, and that maybe there has been a revolution, may it also be said that this art is different from the art of Giotto or the art of Michelangelo — all of which had the same intent, somehow, to convey a message? My answer would be, no. Abstract art and its last manifestation, abstract expressionism, is concerned with man. It is concerned with humanism as much as any art form ever has been, but its means are different. Its means are not immediately "readable."

In the history of art there has been this kind of double statement, one of ideas and the other of feeling. I believe that as the ideas have become more and more minimized, the feeling has, somehow, become more and more maximized. Therefore, what you see today, particularly in abstract expression, is a kind of massive statement of the artist's feeling, and more particularly a massive statement of the artist's personality — good or bad.

You may be indifferent to it, but that is the intent of the communication — in feeling the various responses, the various needs, the character of the artist. This is what it is.

As the artist moved toward abstraction, one might say that all the time he was inerested in exploiting imaginative possibilities. What can the artist do with these inert media — the canvas or the ore mined from the soil of Italy which we call burnt umber, these lifeless things? What can he do to make something living? This was the intent of Monet. It was somehow the passion of Cezanne and Van Gogh, and all the others whom we know so well.

But sometime, say around 1940 or 1950, when we come to the advent of abstract expressionism, we come to an approach to art which radically differs with the art of the past, and perhaps the most important factor here is one of media.

Everyone concerned in the preparation of a "commercial" job goes about it in a certain manner — from thumbnail roughs into a more finished statement and, finally, there is the rendering or the photograph or the finished result. It is an end result of processes.

The most spectacular thing about abstract expressionism is that it is immediate in its conception and immediate in its result. One might say it is the immediate translation of feeling into form.

Sometmes, I know, you are aggravated when you go into a museum and see pictures which look as though they were done in five minutes or even less. And you say, "Can this be taken seriously?" That is because, logically, you are the product of the Renaissance, you are the product of your own way of thinking. Almost, one might say, the product of a Puritan background — that somehow result is equated with effort, with work.

But, for better or worse, the fact is that this new approach to art, this new aim in art, this immediate seizing of feeling cannot be developed on the basis of a long drawn-out thinking process. One must somehow evoke a feeling and then seize it, somehow transform it into its pictorial corollary or symbol.

What I would like to think is that when you see an example of abstract expressionism, it is a communication, it is a symbol, but it is not a symbol the meaning of which was agreed upon previous to the making.

Perhaps I can add something which will seem almost irresponsible to you, and that is that the artist did not know what he was going to make until he had made it. This is radically different, as I have indicated, from your own planning.

One might say that chance, that accident, plays a major role; again, this is simply part of the whole creative process. As we go through the history of art, there are many examples of this "chance." There are artists like Leonardo who indicate that thinking, that deliberation, is not always productive of art. All of you are familiar with what he said about gazing at the discolored wall — instead of seeing the cracks and various discolorations of paint and plaster, the artist sees images, sees mountains, fishes. In fact, we all have that ability to evoke images from some kind of an accidental pictorial complexion.

There is a story about Turner, painting one day in the English countryside. He had his balls of color arranged to paint when he noticed some children nearby who were also painting. Suddenly he got this brilliant idea. Taking his balls of color, he put them down alongside of the children, put out a sheet of watercolor paper, and said to them, "Dip your fingers in the various balls, and just make some kind of an image on the paper" — in other words, at random. The children did so, although they did not know what they were doing. Turner watched them, waited for the watercolors to dry, and then he inserted the various touches of color which would make this into a landscape — into mountains, and skies, into calves and fishes.

I am sure that all of you have done this at sometime or another. All of you have looked at a piece of work upside down and seen in the work possibilities that you didn't know were there when you were thinking deliberately.

What the abstract expressionist is trying to do is simply to exploit this new approach to art, and he does it through a practical application. He is "thinking practical," one might say. He finds that this has worked for him and he finds that the symbol that he has created is evocative of more significance than the picture which he had made in the past.

I think this whole new approach simply incites us to new thinking in terms of the making of these images. You do not see any clear-cut forms. You cannot read these paintings easily. This is in the nature of this new type of art. If one considers the importance of bringing a work of art to life, of seeing it as live, this is what the artist is trying to do. He is trying to energize inert substances and give them a massive semblance of life.

Now, we come to the problem of meaning. All of you are crystal clear about the communication of ideas for the purposes of obvious meanings, but there is another understanding of this term, "meaning." We say philosophically sometimes, all of us, "What is the meaning of our lives? What is the meaning of the work we do? Where are we going? What is the meaning of the kind of social anarchy that the world presents today?"

This "meaning" is somehow correlated to significance. It isn't a meaning which is easily read. Sometimes it seems to me that it has to do almost with an odd kind of meaning, the kind of meaning which is not possible to communicate in words, the meaning which is replete with the deepest kind of impact, the kind of meaning that we see, let us say, when we look out at the Grand Canyon or see a sunset which overwhelms us or when we make love.

How can we speak about the meaning of this? How can we put it into words? Somehow the artist has to contrive a non-discursive symbol, and I would like to say to you that the meaning of all of the great works of the past, all the masterpieces, has never been achieved because of the communication of ideas, it has been achieved by the communication of feelings.

Can you read the various paintings of the Renaissance? Can you read the motivation in a primitive work of art? The answer is, no. But what you can somehow feel communicated is the meaning, the significance. And this is what I believe to be the intent and the purpose and the significance of what we are trying to do in this style called abstract expressionism.

Comments by THE PANELISTS IN ANSWER TO QUESTIONS

QUESTIONS ADDRESSED TO AUSTIN BRIGGS

What can we do about the "bad health" of the illustration profession? What would you recommend?

That is one of those questions on which one could discourse for a long time. But the very important, very obvious, answer which any of you can supply is better work.

It seems to me that most of the people I talk to are kind enough to attempt to lift me up by whatever means they can in the hope that I can perform in a more readily communicative way than I have been able to in the past.

And I feel that, although I don't know all the people who buy work in my aspect of the art world, those I do know are asking this same question of my contemporaries and the newer illustrators, and that a kind of sickness, which is not new, still prevails in the field of illustration. It is a sickness which says they don't really want anything good, they just want what they have been getting or they want this way or they want that way.

To repeat, I think the answer to the ill health of the field is simply better work. Speaking personally, I'm not at all sure that I can do it. I'm being asked to do it, not unkindly I assure you. I am being asked to transcend myself, and I think all the rest of the people who are in the field or who are trying to get in it are being asked to transcend themselves.

If they manage to do it the field will be healthy.

Why are you taking a year off to study painting at this point, at the peak of your career?

It has to do with what I have just stated. I think it is very easy to fall into the attitude that the way you did the picture the last time was all right, because they have called you again and they want you to do another picture.

This is egoism in the extreme, but almost everyone who has been as successful as I have been gets to the point where he thinks he's pretty hot stuff. It is probably the most dangerous state of mind in the world for a commercial artist, which I am. It means that the level one has reached wouldn't be maintained past next week. It cannot stay there. The taste has to be lifted. The imagination has to be moved. The mind and body and spirit have, somehow, to be shaken out of their complacency.

I have felt complacent thousands of times, and realized in the next fleeting second that this was not only my death commercially but my death as a human being. That there was no resting place, and that I shouldn't seek one. If for one moment I found one, I should take myself elsewhere. That 's what I've done.

The series of advertisements for TV Guide *has been running for four years because, I think, Austin Briggs' illustrations never seem to run out of interest. The reason, I found out, is that these illustrations are not done in the artist's studio, and they aren't worked up from imagination but they are actually on-the-spot illustrations drawn in the type of situations that we all find ourselves in. If you were going to sell a picture of a conference room session, let us say, there is something very honest and truthful here, and not always very flattering. That is the reason why this series never seems to get old; there is always a new version of the subject, a new composition, a new interest, new people and so on.*

With this preamble, I wonder if you could give us your thoughts on the business of using photographs versus illustrations in advertising?

Yes, I have some strong feelings on the matter. I once made a speech, which I thought was a pretty good one, and after it was over someone in the audience came up to me and said "great rock throwing."

"How many '62 issues over 8 million?" "All of them."

Advt. No. 430—8¾" x 11¾"
New Yorker—March 13, 1962

Courtesy *TV Guide*

76

My instinct has always been to fight something which, I think, is a challenge. It is rather unfortunate, as far as the rock throwing is concerned, that I happen to admire the work of Art Kane very greatly. As he touched on in the preceding pages, it seems to me that the photograph has been used, and used, and used in its dullest form for practically everything because, I assume, it is easier or quicker or cheaper or requires less thought or less trouble or because the art director can have 50 versions of the same lack of an idea to work from.

I think the photograph has been used so much in advertising, and recently in the editorial pages of publications, that many of us, to use that phrase again, are brainwashed to the point where we assume that what is real is what is photographic, and this just ain't so.

As I have said, it is just as easy to lie with a photograph as it is with a painting or drawing, and in many ways it is easier, in the sense it is easier to make the lie believed because so many people have somehow become conditioned to believing that since it is a photograph, since an image has been made through a mechanical device, this must be a true image of life.

Art Kane, I am sure, would agree with me that it isn't necessarily a true image of life. I'm afraid I've gotten lost a little bit. My hostility is beginning to show on this subject.

To repeat, if I am repeating myself, the photograph is all persuasive, and it is very hard for a painting or a drawing to compete with it in believability if everybody thinks the photograph is the truth and all the rest is a manufactured product.

It seems to me that, to comment on the difference between them, there is a place for the photograph, which the drawing or painting can't fill, and that those people who buy work for such advertisements and magazines should use the photograph in those places. But, when it comes to the other places, they should use the other things.

There has been a rash of stuff in the last few years in advertising which isn't photographic, and down at the bottom you see "Bettmann Archives" printed there. It makes me wonder whether the only thing available is old stuff which has already been manufactured, or photographs, which you can buy in great dullness again.

As Art Kane said, the great photographer, the good photographer, beats the instrument he is using; he manages somehow to express himself through it. He fights his way through it, and on those occasions the photograph is fine. Otherwise it's just a bore to me. I am so sick of seeing them that I almost wish the good ones were gone.

77 *If an advertisement or brochure consists of a happy marriage of words and art, and if, as is often the case, the words and the kernel of the graphic idea are the product of one man's mind, and the elaboration and execution of the art element must be supplied by another talent, how is the necessary collaboration best achieved?*

I must answer that, as in a "real" marriage, there is no pat formula for success. Probably the analogy may be carried farther, however. It is commonly thought, even today, that the best marriages are most often based on a similar background, interests, education, etc., and I believe the fullest success to be derived from the collaboration of the artist and the copy-writer may rise out of the same basic similarities. Certainly, long, tedious explanations of thoughts and ideas are deadly enemies to the formation of a successful advertising message. Really good results arise from a collaboration between creative people who are so attuned to each other's thinking that little consultation is needed. On the other hand (as in some good marriages), there's often no way to beat the "hybrid-vigor" concept. Two creative individuals who fight like hell may come up with the best "brain-child." In the final analysis, the best collaboration is probably the result of brains, talent, experience, intuition and just plain luck.

With the rise of photography and design, and the revision of format and concept of such magazines as Saturday Evening Post, *what do you consider to be the future of communication through realistic illustration?*

If that word "realistic" had quote marks around it, the question would be easier to answer. I don't think we should forget that the "realistic" illustration of today is not the same fish it was yesterday. As my opening statement should have made clear, I don't think all the recent changes are good, but I do believe that some of the realism is more "real" than it was a few years past because of a new awareness of the need for the precise "feeling" as well as the precise "object." In addition, I suggest that you watch the *Post* closely from now on, as I'm sure the "bits and pieces" phase is past, and more communicative pictures are on the way. As for the "ascendancy" of the photograph and design nowadays, we need only to consult past *AD Annuals* to see how the tide waxes and wanes. Granted that the photograph is better than ever, I'm still betting on creativity "sans machine."

Why can't illustrators and photographers make use of some of the emotional structure in a picture, referred to by Mr. McNeil? Don't your pictures contain some abstract design that is planned rather than just happening?

I would be dismayed to find that they did not, since my primary effort is to construct a picture which, in its very structure, expresses the meaning and feeling of the objects (people, things) I put in it. For those who find this statement unacceptable, I suggest another look at my *TV Guide* series.

It is my opinion that illustration such as you do for TV Guide *contains more symbolism than is possible in photographs. When backgrounds and settings are reduced to symbols in photography it seems to me that the picture becomes a phoney. It may carry the message, but it still looks phoney. Isn't this an area where illustration wins the argument about truth and believability hands down? Will you comment on this?*

Perhaps it is too obvious to point out that it is comparatively simple to make a specific point in a painting or drawing without sacrificing "believability," versus the difficulty the photographers must face. The photographic method most widely employed today is to "soft-focus" that portion of the picture least important to the message. The difficulty encountered is that the camera "machine" will not accommodate itself to anything but "focal-planes" of sharpness or obscurity, and what happens to the objects represented when they fall into an undesirable "focal-plane"? The problem is too difficult presently, and probably for the future too, as even the computers still need someone human to formulate the questions. Countless attempts have been made to "illustrate" fiction with photographs (even direction by illustrators), but so far no one seems impressed—except by the unsuitability of the means. In my view, the decisive point is that *the camera cannot synthetize.*

Your TV Guide *series has been called a "classic" campaign. Does this limit your effectiveness in approaching a different sort of problem — say, a cigarette campaign? Would your new ads suggest* TV Guide *to the new audience you would be addressing?*

Superficially, I have suffered from too much success in achieving an identity for an advertiser throughout my career. Actually, the success has been the direct result of single-minded purpose. As I said in my opening statement, I can't forget that the prestige of the people I work for is inseparable from my own. I am not foolish enough to think that my pictures, however memorable, go on remaining identified with past campaigns indefinitely. They fade from vivid memory in all but the most retentive minds as soon as the advertiser decides that the job has been done and the aim achieved. More importantly, they are not the same pictures because the problem to be solved is not the same. At one time it was thought that everything I had to say had been said for Gulf Oil, or American Airlines, or Douglas Aircraft. As time has proved, I have been fortunate enough to be able to invent, exploit and abandon many styles without becoming trapped in one. I have no concept of myself as an artist, nor any preconception to the solution of a picture problem before the problem arises. Both await a challenge.

Would you feel that the abstraction in print advertising done by illustrators tends to frighten the consumer, due to his desire to grasp realism in his insecure existence?

This question calls for a value judgment I'm reluctant to attempt to make. I don't know *why* the consumer is frightened, or whether he's frightened at all, but I do feel that he's put off by a lack of concreteness in the message. I don't think that art can really *be* completely abstract. All forms carry associations and, to me, some so-called abstractions carry rewarding ones, but the public is confused because the associations are so vague and personal. Mr. McNeil said abstractions might be thought of as good or bad, and that we might be indifferent to them. If we may be *indifferent* where is the communication?

QUESTIONS ADDRESSED TO ART KANE

When you accept a photographic commission, just what part of this is a projection of the image you are trying to make and what part of it is trying to get something of yourself in each one of those photographs? Do you seem to be getting yourself in there? What is it you are trying to do?

I suppose part of it has to do with the very reason I made the switch from art directing to photography to begin with, and a lot of it also has to do with ego.

Not believing in specialization, I have been working in many, many different areas but I have avoided, we'll say, fashion per se or the selling of the garment, because this is one area where I feel it's rather difficult for me to come through. I feel that unless I were passionate about clothing and women as, we'll say, Richard Avedon is, I could never make a personal statement in Suzy Parker — she would wind up being the star of the picture, and not me. In that sense it is ego.

As far as the transition from art direction into photography, it was a tremendous passion for the medium that had developed over a period of years. I had started taking pictures about 10 or 11 years ago. I have been a professional photographer for about two years in all—devoting full time to it.

Over the period of time when I was sharing my work between art direction and photography, the interest in photography as a medium was getting stronger and stronger; the interest in design per se was getting less and less.

Then there was the decision of going into this medium, having to depend on it for a living, having to feed my wife and two children. Would I be able to maintain the same cockiness, so to speak, of accepting or rejecting a job according to my own evaluation of it when my livelihood depended on it? Before I went into it full-time, if I would receive an assignment that did not meet with my own demands or did not interest me, I would say "Sorry, but I'm not interested." It was easy. I didn't depend on the money for a living.

So there was a tremendous decision about whether I could maintain this integrity, if you want to call it that, or whether I would go into it as a business. In other words, was I going to be more of the artist and more concerned with self-expression in what I had to say or was I going to be Art Kane Photography Studio, Inc., which is a rather disgusting title I have to cling to?

I decided then and there that I was not going to leave a good position and a fairly good reputation as an art director, and a steady salary every week, to go into photography and become bored with it. I did not want to lose this great love.

So, I decided at that point that if I entered into it, more or less on my terms, I would try to produce pictures as I saw them, without being too hot-headed about it because I did (and do) realize also my responsibility to the client. On the other hand I realized that it would be absolutely necessary for me to work only for those clients who understood what I do, and who have enough respect for it to warrant my services with a minimum of deviation.

In that sense I have not accepted, and to this day will never accept, an assignment that I do not feel is right. I will very quickly recommend someone else. I feel it is unfair both to the client and to myself to produce a photograph someone else could do with more passion and with more interest.

I was scared silly when I made the transition, because I did not know whether I would be able to make a go of it or not, but I have. And I suppose, in that sense, I am working or I am more concerned with maintaining my imagery than I am with simply creating a photograph for commercial purposes.

Can photography be reaching its importance as an aid to advertising because of any underlying need for images the consumer can readily accept as real?

As a rule people do not buy blindly. We like to *see* what we're buying before we make a decision for or against. The more information we receive in this preview stage the better we like it. This has nothing to do with art, simply information. On this level there's no question that a photographic image, being closer to reality than the painted image, is more readily accepted by the consumer public.

Photography has always made advances in other areas of advertising where realism is not at all desired. Here, in fact, is the area that I personally function in more so than the other. Photography has proven itself not only as the medium for recording realistic images but also a medium of interpretive images — the difference between the poet and the newspaper reporter. Therefore, once again the area previously confined to the painter-illustrator has been infiltrated by photography.

Practically all photos in the Metropolitan Museum of Art's "Fine Arts" photo show are by professional photographers. The first show, two or three years ago, had one *photo by an amateur. Did you mean to say that in your opinion these shows were "amateurish" — not by amateurs?*

I merely meant to dramatize the point that photography, being a mechanical medium and one available to any and all living creatures, can accidentally produce a work of high artistic quality. Therefore, if even *one* work produced by an amateur has appeared in a show at the Metropolitan, it is highly indicative. We must learn to evaluate the difference between a photograph and a body of work. If a photograph is good, we must respect it as an image; but we must always be conscious of whether the camera or the *man* took the picture.

82 QUESTIONS ADDRESSED TO HENRY KOERNER

Is not abstract expression some means of escaping the rigorous disciplines of the more objective means of expression? How can abstract expression be judged as to its worth if the disciplines are difficult to define?

A Persian rug, a calligraphy from the Koran, a carved ornament from the Alhambra or from a Gothic cathedral, a bentwood chair, a wrought-iron gate, a china plate, a type face — each wields hypnotic power. For example, the Hebrew letters, black on white, are characterized by strongly emphasized dark and heavy horizontals of earth and the earth-bound man; by searching, weightless verticals of air and spiritually freed man; and by 45-degree angles of growing man and nature — all orchestrated together with flame wave-shaped Baroque wholeness.

Abstract expressions are matched by the other side of the coin that bears a more objective means of man's expression. Here are the storytellers of religious, heroic and symbolic subject matter — the portraitists, satirists, naturalists and realists, who run the gamut from the romantic-sentimental to the naked-brutal.

When the two faces of this coin can merge into one image, when a non-objectivity and an objectivity are joined inseparably, then we are confronted with a seeming impossibility — a true miracle, a masterpiece, such as a Giotto, a Breughel or a Cezanne.

These are the definitions. There is no possible escape from them, only the attempt to escape.

"Girl Queen"
Courtesy Midtown Galleries

Courtesy Howard Wise Gallery

QUESTIONS ADDRESSED TO GEORGE McNEIL

Would you explain one of your pictures, please?

The painting, "Nike," was begun in late 1955 and finished in 1959. I can identify it because it was one of the first of "square" (48″ x 48″), or just off a square, sizes that I've been using since then. This relates to my working method since I improvise, letting the form and color relations, themselves, dictate further developments. To secure greater visual stimulation, I keep turning the pictures in the same direction, so that there is no "up" or "down" while I'm painting. I decided on a square or abstract square size since this increased the possibilities for form and color to jell in any position of the canvas.

Like most of the paintings made since 1950, "Nike" had a random beginning; that is, movements of color were laid on without any representational or ideational referents. Then a trial-and-error process evolved where always the effort was to elicit artistically meaningful forms. To keep my sensitivity keen and alert, I worked on many pictures simultaneously, say seven or eight. As these were visible all the time, sudden flashes or intuitions often came from turning from one picture and suddenly seeing the need for a color-form or movement in another picture. Thus, it was with "Nike." I recall that after about three years of intermittent work and despairing of ever finishing it, I suddenly saw the need to simplify its "background," and with a four- or five-inch brush, filled with paint intended for another canvas, I quickly struck in a large area and, for me, the painting was finished.

This non-sequential method may disturb those who like to plan their work, say in terms of representational images or in the controlled manner of a Mondrian. My way may seem irresponsible. But, I've done both and have, in the past, not only painted realistically but have also made precise abstractions. I find that this method works for me, that it's practical, that I get better work. And in the end, that's what counts; the proof of any painting method must be realized in the painting.

What standards do you use to evaluate your communication's effectiveness? How do you know *you are communicating?*

There are no real standards which can be used to judge the effectiveness of artistic communication when the work of art is created. Only time *really* determines the effectiveness of any art and, even so, there are ups and downs of artistic acceptance. Raphael, for example, so admired in the late 19th century, is rarely held as a paragon today. This applies also to Sargent, considering a more recent "famous" artist. Conversely, Cezanne was almost completely rejected about 50 years ago while today he is linked with masters such as Michelangelo, Rembrandt and Goya.

An artist can only respond to his own convictions and artistic integrity, and hope that communication will occur. He cannot consider the level of his audience and modify his art to insure communication. And then, too, what about the different audiences for art? One cannot expect to communicate with a tabloid reader if one is aiming at absolutes of artistic expression.

I am forced to think deliberately when I view an abstract composition with a title below it such as "Confused City No. 15." If the reason for this form of art is some sort of visual delight, why do these artists make us search out a message?

Don't seek out a message, especially with abstract paintings; let the painting evoke a reaction, or perhaps no reaction at all. Important here is an openness of receptivity, of looking at a given piece over a period of time. In visiting a museum, one might slowly walk by the pictures and stop at those that are appealing. Often, you will find that "indifferent" or even "hated" works will beguile themselves into appreciation, will ultimately become meaningful.

The difficulty here is trying to "read" or decipher abstractions in terms of the titles which usually have nothing to do with the picture's motivation. They are only names, identifying signs, the way children, pets or race-horses are named. Usually, *after* the work is finished, it is named. We are so accustomed to reading the story in our traditional representational art, of interpreting really, that we carry the same habit to abstract art which manifestly communicates feeling rather than ideas.

So, in conclusion, consider the title as a handle or identification, and don't let it influence your response to the immediacy of the form and color.

Were not some of the gargoyles in little-known places in cathedrals some form of abstract art?

Throughout the history of art, artistic imagination has fostered many strange, non-realistic art-forms. This was a "side activity" done for the personal satisfaction of the artists, done at the same time that they were creating official or socially-accepted realistic art, say in the Gothic era, the head of a saint. The gargoyles were not part of any religious practice, and were not readily visible to the lower classes or their art-buying masters and, hence, the stonecarvers were free to let their fancy go and create what, to us, is almost "Surrealism." This also happened with carvings beneath the seats of choir-stalls where vulgar and ribald scenes were often depicted. Always the desire of artists to break through social and artistic conventions has operated; today the "anything goes" of much contemporary art is simply the most untrammeled art expression of this traditional longing for new forms.

There seems to be a trend among non-objective painters to paint bigger *and* bigger *canvases. Do they feel that this makes the work more important? Or do they need this big space for "freer expression" in brushstrokes, spontaneity, etc.? Or is it because the same painting made larger can be sold for a higher price?*

Several motives are involved in the large abstraction trend. Most important, the freedom for great movements of color-forms, the so-called "action painting" of abstract expressionism, calls for large, directly stated areas. It's the difference between the finger movement of more traditional painting and the total body movements of much expressionism. Then too, there is the challenge presented by large sizes; once involved in working large on canvases, it's hard to be satisfied with small dimensions. Also operative is the salon concept where, in exhibitions, a large picture attracts more attention than a small one.

Of course, finally, the size of the art work has little to do with ultimate value. A genuine artist can realize his artistic convictions on a 10 by 12 inch canvas as well as upon one of 10 by 12 feet.

QUESTIONS ADDRESSED TO THE PANEL IN GENERAL

Is it not true that what you are all seeking (in common) is not just an "expression" by each medium but that the end result should be both interesting and evocative instead of "reporting," regardless of the method used to get it? This *would elevate the end results above mediocrity.*

Comments by ART KANE

Honest reporting is not akin to mediocrity. I have as much respect for the reporter who photographs the woman plunging from the hotel window or the flag raising at Iwo Jima as for those involved in going beyond pure realism. Both schools of thought are necessary — one for pure and unadulterated information, the other for capturing the essence of things. One tells us what happened. The other makes us feel or experience the happening.

Comments by HENRY KOERNER

Each person is a unique, unrepeatable and irreplaceable singularity, seeking his very own expression and realization of his being God-like. Religious, philosophical, political or esthetic systems may help his problem. But only through *great art* can man again and again be uniting, liberating and communicative to man and his living god. The great artist is always a reporter with limitless insight, will and skill. He is a field marshal, turning each state of being from the changing into the changeless. This he does in a contest and a discourse with, and a longing for, the "Thou."

Words like "interesting" and "evocative" are meaningless when applied to Beethoven's Ninth Symphony or Melville's *Moby Dick.* Those judging art in these terms are covering up blindness. Frequently the response to a masterwork is another masterwork. And thus civilization prospers and grows, springing and sparking from one inspiration to another.

87 Comments by GEORGE MCNEIL

That the "end result should be both interesting and evocative" is, of course, a desideratum of all artists. However, almost all useful art is circumscribed by commercial motives and the test of advertising art ultimately must be the sale of the advertised product or service. Thus, an ultimate goal of all concerned with education is to raise the standards of the public so that well-designed art will be demanded. Then, the limited instrumental character of much contemporary design can be replaced by the desire of all artists — that is, an ultimate in quality.

Does the panel recognize any danger in "over-communication"? Could the result be that inherent differences are lost? Too much "formula"?

Comments by ART KANE

We are unquestionably victims of over-communication. We live under the influence of communication in its many guises from moment to moment, every day of our lives. We are being hypnotized into a state of subconscious desire for material things through this "over-communication." The millions of repetitive statements in repetitive ads in repetitive publications have become part of our lives. We make jokes about it, but we can't seem to stop it.

There is no difference between the professional hypnotist — dangling a shiny object before our eyes and repeating over and over again his demands — and the ritual of selling cigarettes, under-arm deodorants or Vic Tanney's on television screens or in magazine ads. The approach is similar, and the results are probably identical. Both persuade you into subconscious action. One merely takes a bit longer than the other.

Comments by HENRY KOERNER

The only danger to man is his death-wish. We have witnessed in our time the most hideous crime man has ever known, Germany's death camps, and now, ever hovering over our worlds, is dread of total annihilation by the "Bomb."

All the while, weightless, mindless, imprisoned man seeks escape in outer space, to search the realm of science-technology for the answer to his know-nothingness. And now many artists themselves seek a formula for communication. Only love, deep-rooted ties with nature and great art reassure man's will to live as he experiences the joy and pride of being alive in the flesh.

 Writes Alexander Eliot, author-editor, master of insight: "Turn from the pit. We know how to turn away, you and I, from known pits at least, and the poisoned meat that baits them. Come away with me, into the forests of being. Let them have their cities of becoming, and their circuses that build a horror in the brain. It is yet possible to love mankind from a distance, with dignity, like the wild lion musing on his mountain ledge. The true beast is no beast's creature, though he be in danger. The darkness wins most of the massed battles, the light wins most individual ones. Let us yet skirmish from the forest, like lions of golden light."

Comments by GEORGE MCNEIL

If by "over-communication" is meant pandering to mass-audiences, the well-known, twelve-year old mass mentality, then of course, formulas, clichés and similar stereotyped, i.e., non-creative, designs and illustrations are almost inevitable. You may say that Giotto and the later Renaissance masters worked creatively for the mass audiences of the church. If there ever was any truth in art being a visual catechism for the people, a popular mass art certainly isn't around now. Witness the average Hollywood movie which, directed to mass audiences, is almost inevitably banal and mediocre.

How much draftsmanship or background study of the basic knowledge of drawing is necessary to a true abstract artist? Or is this often the "happy accident" school of art?

Comments by HENRY KOERNER

Drawing is everything — from the athlete's coordination of eye, body, arm and hand that holds the pen or brush to the coordination of the intellect that draws everything together into the meaning or the total vision. The greatest painters have also been the greatest draftsmen and greatest thinkers.

In the drawing we can *see* the paradox between the easily recognizable object and the completely unrecognizable abstract forces that constitute this object. The drawing demonstrates the master's simultaneous acceptance of his absolute truthfulness and his belief in art, which he knows to be an untruth, an illusion. In this sense, the drawings by a Dürer, a Vermeer, or a Pissarro are fundamentally different from the sketching or rendering of a Henry Moore, a Picasso, a Klee, a Mondrian or a Dali.

89 Comments by GEORGE MCNEIL

A whole new attitude is needed in relation to the means and ends of abstract art. Draftsmanship and basic knowledge of drawing were necessary when artists, however much concerned with expressiveness, had to communicate ideas. This is given by the whole history of art from the early Egyptians to about 1900. Then, in almost every instance, art was utilized for religious, governmental or other social purposes and, hence, figures and other forms had to be convincingly real. Some artists still communicate these ideas and, hence, they too must know how to draw. Others, interested in abstract (i.e., non-representational, non-figurative) modes of expression, have no need for traditional drawing. Would an atomic age scientist be required to know Euclidean concepts of space, concepts not needed for this post-Einstein era? Perhaps yes, but only as background knowledge. Something of the same is true of draftsmanship and correct drawing. It would be nice for young artists to be able to draw realistically, but this accomplishment would be irrelevant to their paramount interest in making the totality of form and color expressive.

If you could specify the use of a substantial fund for basic research in visual communication (at universities, research institutes or art schools, for example), what would be the principal areas or questions you would want studied?

Comments by HENRY KOERNER

If I could specify the use of a substantial fund for basic research in visual communication, the principal area I would want studied is the possibility of the invention of an "Art Meter," that, if held towards a given artwork, would tell those partially or totally blind art critics, museum directors, art directors, art collectors and "art lovers" if the artwork were good or bad. Or perhaps it could be pointed at you or me to test our own artistic sincerity and integrity.

Comments by GEORGE MCNEIL

As to research in visual communication, my attitude is somewhat negative. I don't believe that there are any standard design solutions, and research directed toward fixed or absolute preferences — for example, that smokers prefer white packages — can only be significant for short periods of time (while the "white package" is fashionable) and can only lead to design atrophy. Basic to any art concept is the continual search for new form, new visual excitement; any absolutes, such as were given in "dynamic symmetry" and other art systems are bound to become artistically bankrupt. So, in short, the kind of research that I'm interested in is that which would indicate that there are no simple, fixed solutions, no easy ways, that finally one's creative imagination must determine those form and color relations which give us art.

U. S., us
yardstick of progress in visual communication

GEORGE NELSON
President, George Nelson & Co., Inc., Industrial Design

What is the Face of America? A gash, like the Grand Canyon? An excrescence, like the Rocky Mountains? The Washington Monument — the Wrigley Building — Freedomland? In our search for an answer, it was apparent from the beginning that the material was too rich. A Disney might cope with it, but no ordinary person. We therefore sifted, and weighed, and chose, and eliminated, and came up with a three-point decision. We decided to limit our exploration to three of the most conspicuous features in our landscape: the places in which people live and where they shop were the first two choices, for both the dwelling and Main Street are inescapable, no matter where one goes.

In looking at these great market places and at the millions of little shrines of togetherness, one vital piece of information communicated itself very rapidly: there is no variation. Everything everywhere is just like everything everywhere else. We are the first society in history to so arrange things that the population can move rapidly and endlessly from one city to another and still remain, so to speak, in exactly the same place.

Having made these two choices, a feeling developed that there was now enough architecture. We therefore picked as our third category something we also see everywhere and all the time: the product. It is with us at home, on the road, in the office, in outer space, on the beach.

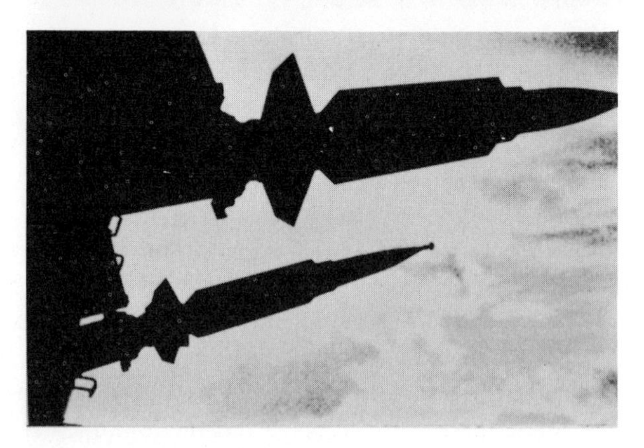

The Small Consumer Product (top) borrows shapes from
The Large Consumer Product (center), which gets its ideas from
The Master Product (bottom), the originating source for forms.

93 *The Product*

The first group of products we shall look at represents nothing that is going to be new to any of us. They are small consumer products; they are things we can buy at the store and take home.

The characteristics of this group are very interesting. They are, on the whole, weak in design, imitative, derivative, highly styled, rarely designed in the basic sense of the word and, as far as we can discover, generally lacking in anything that can be described as integrity.

These are products that are made for the direct use of people, and they fall into a number of styles and categories. There are the architectural approaches to this kind of thing, and there are the high-speed or dynamic approaches. In the case of one product, for instance, the decision to make what might be symmetrical unsymmetrical obviously creates a sense of displacement; this thing is moving. In case the consumer is too dopey to figure this out from the design itself, there is a familiar airplane symbol in the upper left-hand corner which repeats the point.

We live in a dynamic period. Movement is one of the things that tends to stimulate and excite us, and the product has to *move*. If it moves at a slow rate, something must be done to the styling to at least increase the visual miles-per-hour. And it is characteristic of the successful small consumer product that it says very clearly that it is going somewhere with a purpose, with great thrust, and in a hurry.

The little products, of course, look to the bigger products for their cues. And the little product, whatever it is, is obviously looking with admiration on its big brothers and sisters produced by Detroit. There are exhausts, there are intakes, there are all sorts of things to enable the weak little product to look strong like the bigger ones. Of course, if the product uses jet propulsion it is that much easier to achieve complete success.

The second group we are going to look at is also completely familiar to all. These are consumer products, too, but they are big. These are also bought in stores, but you cannot put them in .shopping bags. Here we can see where many of the ideas used with such admiration and respect by the little products are exposed on a much bigger scale.

One could go on for a long time studying some of the sculptural problems which have been given expression in these larger products. We are all familiar with them, but one of the curious things about the large consumer product group is that it too, like the little ones, looks somewhere else.

What we find is that while the automobile tends to give the lead in product styling to the great mass of small consumer products, it also is not quite sure of itself. So it, in turn, looks to what we might call a group of master products.

One of the interesting characteristics of these products in both the large and small consumer categories is that they have been designed *not* to age well.

Among other large consumer products, things like boats have become conspicuous since the war. Unlike the automobile, which looks to jets, rockets and so on, the boat is trying to look like the automobile. And it is quite intriguing to see how boats have willingly, in the interest of better design for the consumer, given up their look of "boatliness" and are taking on the automotive look. If one can get out of a car into a boat which is exactly like a car, perhaps — I don't know — perhaps one feels more at home.

Then, of course, there are intermediate large consumer products, some of them interesting composites of different trains of thought — one, for instance, on which the top says Grand Prix racing car while the bottom says tractor.

Again, there is the large group known as home appliances. You get a much more restrained approach here because these things are really nailed down; you cannot put wheels on them. Where they do relate to other large consumer products is in their emphasis on controls. To turn on our electric stoves one would think it would take just a switch or a button, but the housewife is presented with something more like the flight deck of the Caravelle. Maybe this has political, or even military, implications.

Status has come to this product group. All sorts of beautiful things happen. The feeling that you get in the new kitchens is that Mama can put on her Dior evening dress in the morning and work in it through the whole day. This is better than the kind of drudgery that our parents and grandparents were subjected to. However, there is also an attempt to blend the machine approach to things with the cozy, homey, togetherness type of approach which, if it doesn't develop schizophrenia, at least gives the architect who designed the kitchen something to think about.

Every period has what one might call "master" products. These are the products on which the society of that era will lavish the largest amounts of money, because this represents an expression of its belief in the most direct and powerful way. Here we find that designers in the conventional sense — the industrial designer's sense — have pretty much disappeared from the scene. But the design itself has become absolutely breathtaking.

In these products we are dedicated, without exception, to impersonal,

The Small Consumer Product: It is generally at the low end of the People/Product Scale. Success appears to come most readily to those products which look as though they were going somewhere in a hurry. For example, the electric shaver (right), an essentially symmetrical object, moves in the direction in which its case has been sculpted. To make sure you get the idea, an airplane wings across its nameplate in the same direction.

The slide viewer (left) and portable mixer (right) look like parts from a jet engine,

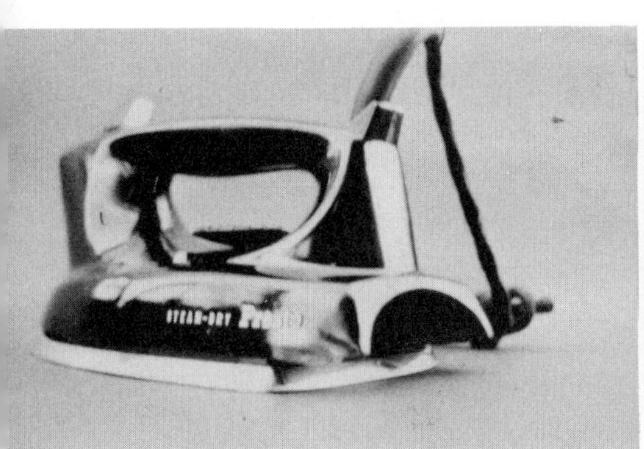

while the carpet sweeper (right) moves across the floor like a wide track car.

abstract notions like movement or power. You rarely see any mistakes. You also never see imitative forms. The variety of forms in this category is beyond belief, and the authenticity of the forms is at a very high level. These things, in a pretty clear way, tell one exactly what they think they're doing.

Big architecture should be listed as part of the master products group, because architecture is in the process of conversion from a kind of artist's handicraft vision of building to something that you can pull out of a catalogue, and the anti-personal expression in our best buildings is very clear.

Not too long ago I walked down Park Avenue past the Seagram Building, and was startled to see the figure of a person at a window on the 11th or 12th floor. I was shocked, and the thought crossed my mind, "What will Mies van der Rohe think?" And I realized that the most truthful expression made by these buildings may be coming presently when the people have been totally eliminated and replaced by data processing systems.

All of our best product-type architecture is *anti-people* or, at least, non-people. In the Air Force Academy, where there is a space nothing human could cover on foot, the things that do cover it are made to walk as if they weren't human, but semi-robot attachments to the planes the boys are learning to fly. The same is true of some factories. The category which is tenderly cared for and moved around very, very carefully is *things,* not people. People walk out on the snow and catch cold. Another curious facet of this architectural type of product is indicated by the garden court of Lever House on Park Avenue where, after years and years of pumping in a great deal of talent, money and all that, nobody has been able to figure out what to do with the space. The reason is that it is for people, and *we have lost the talent of designing for people.*

Incredible, spectacular stuff, every bit of it, whether it be miniaturized components or huge turbines. When it comes to building an automotive-type machine for moving dirt, we can do it and do it beautifully — it comes out a ravishing object. Give the same designer the problem of a machine to move people and it comes out a flashy piece of junk.

The Master Product: Only the products in this category generate original forms as they need them. This is true of a giant highway system or air terminal as well as of a jet transport.

Since an earthmover is usually better designed than a passenger car, it appears that we think moving dirt more important than moving people.

Although they develop different types of forms, Big Arms and Big Architecture are alike in their disregard for people. A Terrier missile eliminates them in a total sense; the Seagram building or Air Force Academy would like to eliminate them in a design sense.

98 *Main Street*

Let us now imagine ourselves riding in a gas-driven, four-wheeled product. We are heading for a city we have not visited before. There is a suggestion of excitement in the air — perhaps it is a feast day in this town we are coming to, a great national holiday like the Fourth of July or Father's Day, or maybe a tremendous commercial orgy, like Christmas.

The road we are on will, of course, take us to the heart of town, where our car will find many other cars to nuzzle. We have all seen Main Street before, but there is always something fascinating about it — its ruggedly individualistic shops and signs, its compulsive congestion, its ersatz vitality.

The people go every day
To Main Street
And buy
Nationally advertised products
On time
To fill their needs
And
To keep American Industry Going
They buy
On time
To maintain
The Living American Living Standard
Of Living
The people
Nuts
And bolts
And boots
Also nutcrackers
Crackers
Ketchup
Cars
And kiddiecars
Home magazines
Which tell them what else to buy
Like maybe canaries
Or electric can openers
Hi-Fi sets
With low fidelity

99

Television sets
With a full five-day guarantee . . .
On time
Ten dollars down
Down Down Down
They buy Wheaties
Posties
Crispies Soggies Creepies
Crunchies Shreddies
Snappies Snackies
And their daily bread

The people who buy the bread take it home, of course, where they put it into the freezer. Home is where we put our daily bread into the freezer.

Home

Home is where we Americans live — God's people. Let us not deny that we are important people — we have only to ignore an advertising campaign and Madison Avenue crumbles. We own more than $25 billion of installment debt. What if we all suddenly decided not to pay? Can you imagine what we would do to the bankers? We are important, indeed. We BUY. The great American miracle is that we can do it without money.

We are terribly important. The giant corporations send out endless teams of skilled researchers to ask us what they should make, and in how many colors, and how much it should cost:

> Dear Mrs. Smith, Do you think that 44 beans in a cup of coffee would be better than 43? Should our company logotype read from right to left, or upside down? Are jets dangerous? Would you like your next car to have five wheels? Would you feel that it was OK, madam, if your husband shot the neighbors when they tried to get into your fallout shelter? What if your neighbor, having seen more television shows, were faster on the draw than your husband, and shot him? Would you be willing to leave the shelter to collect the insurance? Or should the company send it to you? Would you object if the check arrived in a radioactive envelope? How do you feel about 79-octane gas, Mr. Jones, compared to the regular 80? Would you pay more if it were attractively packaged? Do you think Abraham Lincoln was a Fascist? And why, incidentally, do you feel that Kiwanis does more good for the Community than Rotary? Did you or did you not get sexually stimulated when you came to page

211 in *Tropic of Cancer?* Have you any opinions regarding the 5-hour work week? When was the last time you laughed out loud?

We have behind us a splendid tradition of good living: There *are* flowers in our gardens which are not plastic.

We *do* have a tradition of rich and dignified living. There was a breed of men in this country who felt vigorously linked to other, older cultures.

Even where they show the signs of advancing age, there *are* beautiful old dwellings, sensitively designed, full of grace and serenity. To be sure, it has become the fashion to spit on these old relics — and real estate values have taken precedence over other values.

There *was* a love for, and understanding of, the meaning of ornament. There *was* a genuine delight in richness, in the adornment of simple, necessary things. The detail was not always correct, in the pedant's sense, but it was joyful and exuberant and fanciful.

The experiments of our architects today have the respectful attention of the world, though the public generally finds them freakish.

Is it possible that our people do not take pride in our tradition, and derive courage from our experiments?

Epilogue

Pictures could be selected in staggering numbers to show evidence of the most massive production of ugliness in all recorded history. They could also raise disquieting questions — what manner of people did this, are *continuing* to do this?

"What are we supposed to do now — slit our throats?" I was once asked after a discussion about these things.

Americans, like other people, grow up with attitudes. Ours include a belief that action is preferable to thought. We have always tended to do things first and then look surprised at the mess afterwards. Why should we slit our throats? It would make more sense to clean up the mess. Except that we don't do things that way. We look for another campsite where we can make a new mess. The trouble is that we are running out of fresh ground.

We like to think of ourselves as practical people. But we are not practical at all — we are merely anti-intellectual, which is why, when we get into a jam we never stop to think how we got there, but demand, imperiously and impatiently, that we be given "workable" answers. What do we do when there are no workable answers?

101 The reason one can take pictures of those creeping horrors called "Main Street" and "Home" is that they are there. The reason they are there is that the nation has been so busy chasing whatever it is chasing that human values are being largely junked. Colonial America, with much less sophistication and know-how than our own time, produced no such monumental messes. Can we go back to the outlook of 1776? Of course not. Can we look at our current distorted values and change them? We cannot, except as rare individuals: the social pressures are too great.

The next move, perhaps, would be to listen to the politicians and the newspaper and magazine editors when we are exhorted to defend "our way of life" from something or other. The question to be asked is, "What way of life?"

I look at "Main Street," and what it symbolizes, and I have no desire to defend it. I look at the housing developments and I don't want to defend them either. I look at the famed American standard of living and wonder just how much it really has to do with *living*. Some, no doubt, but mostly what one sees is pressure, anxiety, installment debt and traffic jams on weekends. I do not want any child of mine to consider his life a success because he has sold an overpriced power mower to an uninformed customer. I am unable to believe that the Organization Man is an improvement over Neanderthal Man. I do not want any part of Suburbia or Exurbia.

This is a portion of my list. You might enjoy making your own. It is comforting to discover how many things one does not want to support or defend. There is nothing negative about rejection.

Another antidote to pessimism is perspective. Nothing lasts forever. Our time is a very old one, as these things go. It began with the crack-up of the medieval world, and during its young years (which we label the Renaissance) it produced one genius, one masterpiece after another. It reached its maturity in the 18th century, began to run out of gas in the middle of the 19th century, and it finally got on the toboggan in August of 1914. Some people say 1918, but when you are dealing with a period of some five centuries, four years more or less don't make much difference.

There are a number of interesting things one can do at a moment like this. One is to enjoy the tremendous spectacle and try to understand it — which is difficult. The other is to try to figure out what is growing up out of the disintegration of a great culture, and to latch on to it — which is also difficult. Why, for instance, the current international fascination with the esthetic — or symbolic — meaning of junk? The easy move is to join the Cassandras and wail over the impending end of this or that world, but it is really very silly. Can one imagine Michelangelo weeping into his beard over the collapse of the Middle Ages? For him and his contemporaries it was the best thing that ever happened. Perhaps our grandchildren — always assuming that we handle our radioactive toys with reasonable care — will feel the same way.

the need for trained artists in communication

SILAS H. RHODES
Founder and Director,
School of Visual Arts

The exodus of the class of '62 from the colleges, universities and professional schools all over the country has begun. Eagerly, the not so-silent, not so-conservative generation of lawyers, doctors, architects, engineers, business men, teachers and artists are taking up the tasks of their first positions.

The artist-graduate, unlike his contemporaries in science, architecture, engineering and medicine, is not chosen for his first position because of the courses he has taken or the examinations he has passed or the grades he has received or the license requirements he has fulfilled. These criteria of selection for him are irrelevant. It is not too strong to state that he is selected in spite of any evidence of academic respectability. The decisive factor for him in obtaining employment is the contents of a big, black bag, euphemistically referred to as a portfolio, which he carries about in the manner of an itinerant peddler. In the portfolio, arranged as attractively as possible, are samples of his work which purport to show whether the graduate "knows his stuff" and can use his knowledge effectively in his profession. Some portfolios feature shining examples of technique, mistakenly labeled "craftsmanship," while others concentrate on displaying clever solutions to visual problems, mistakenly labeled "originality."

When the graduate takes his portfolio around to art directors, designers and other buyers of art who are also prospective employers, he usually receives, as all beginners must, his fair share of criticism. And if the criticism of the class of '62 runs true to form, it will sound something like this.

> The portfolio is too far out or not far out enough; lacks mastery of skills or is too cluttered with evidence of skills; not enough creative solutions or too many creative but impractical solutions; doesn't communicate or communicates with clichés; no evidence of drawing ability or too much drawing and not enough design; lack of photographic solutions; too many type solutions; too much color or not enough black and white; too much emphasis on taste or not enough awareness of contemporary fashion; not enough grounding in reproduction methods; too many examples of color separation and mechanicals; no evidence of being able to work under pressure — and a myriad host of other contradictory assessments.

Now let me hasten to add that I am in no way objecting to these criticisms. Although, collectively, they may sound confusing, there is little doubt that when applied to individual cases, they have validity. Neither am I objecting to the use of the portfolio as a valid instrument of selection. What I am suggesting is that the preparation of the artist for art direction should be based on a deeper appreciation of the complexity and importance of art education and on a broader concept of an artist's "stuff" than what seems to be implied in these criticisms. And a broader concept of the artist's "stuff" leads to an examination of what his education should be.

Objectives of art education

From art directors, as representatives of an industry which requires immediate results from its acts, one hears about technical, visual competence as the objective of art school education. And the schools, in attempting to satisfy the industry they serve, are forgetting the function of education, particularly the function of a school. The difference between a school — and this distinction includes a professional school like the School of Visual Arts — and all other institutions of society is that the kinds of organized experiences the student receives depend on the kind of man he is to become, not only on the kind of job he is to hold.

Education is a moral affair and the ultimate concern of the school is with moral values, while society is concerned with such matters indirectly and only occasionally. But the school serves to recreate and transmit moral values to each generation anew. That is why the school must mirror the best aspects of society and strive to omit the worst. Hence, an education which devotes itself primarily to the achievement of vocational competence on the part of its students neglects too much. It deprives the student during his last period of organized study of those sensuous experiences which will enable him to quicken to new interests and new appreciations on the way to self-education, which is a life work never ended. To do otherwise is to sacrifice the student to the single track mind. For man's mind is his glory and his intellectual powers distinguish him from other creatures. But the single track mind makes a bore of the art school graduate, distorts his vision and robs him of his selfhood. It prevents him from performing the double tasks which should be required of all students. He must learn "to do something useful for his society and his fellow men" and learn "to know the range of possible human experience, that is, create in himself a rich inner life, stocked with ideas and facts, which are his own and which elevate the person and release him from ignorance and error." (Taylor)

And he, for example, cannot postpone his understanding of the art of communication until he can afford the price of admission to a meeting which will include the observations of Professor Hayakawa about *Language in Thought and Action.* The student needs to read and digest the views of Hayakawa and others while attending school, but not on some odd, rainy afternoon.

By and large, art schools have tended to ignore the moral and intellectual implications of education, while art directors — who, incidentally, when at the top of their form, function as teachers in the best traditions of teaching, since they must do what all good teachers do: evoke the highest quality output from the individual potential being worked with — have not always remembered the moral and intellectual implications of art.

But the singular distinction between the art director and the artist-teacher is that the latter must, in addition, penetrate to the individual core of his students, strip bare the clichés and slogans which insulate the public mind and inspire them to achieve a life style filled with spontaneous and vivid insights. Out of these spontaneous and vivid insights will come their own personal truths and personal values.

For "the 19th century," says Jacques Barzun, the caretaker of the house of intellect, has "plunged us without warning into an industrial culture, and people are still floundering . . . moreover, the dislocation of mechanization and war leaves them bewildered in their intimate lives."

 The need for trained artists

And I find it mildly irritating that at a time when we sorely need trained artists in communication we are not getting them. For the next 40 years we are going to be living in a crowded, scientific, spherical, fast-moving world. Some of the thorniest problems of our world will be: living side by side with people who think differently from us; designing new forms of social and political structure thrust upon us by the increasing complexities of technology and communication; firming up our religions and philosophies to a continually changing science; preserving individuality in the inevitable drift toward conformity through bigness; raising the general level of esthetic appreciation; and learning to make wise use of increased leisure by satisfying work.

At this point, it is rewarding to reflect on the proposition which says that "whatever we do we are supposed to do for the sake of making a living." But, as Hannah Arendt, in her remarkable book *The Human Condition,* has pointed out, "the only exception" to this proposition "society is willing to grant is the artist, who strictly speaking is the only 'worker' left in a laboring society." And the only impulse left to the artist is the impulse to esthetic play which develops into creative art.

On the same point Norman Brown, in *Life Against Death,* has said that "history is transforming the question of reorganizing human society and human nature in the spirit of play from a speculative possibility to a realistic necessity. The most realistic observers are emphasizing man's increasing alienation from his work; the possibility of mass unemployment — i.e., liberation from work — given by modern technology; and the utter incapacity of human nature as it is today to make genuinely free use of leisure — to play."

If the artist is the only worker left in a laboring society and the work of the fine artist has already dissolved into play and lost its worldly meaning, then the work of the art director, the popular art of our time, becomes the new landscape. And if much of his work is only transitory, the cumulative effects of its quality for good or ill pervade the atmosphere.

Yet during this age of alienation we have been willing to settle for training technicians for advertising rather than educating artists for communication. Small wonder that the profession of art direction is not accepted as seriously as it should be, nor the contribution it makes and can make to popular art fully understood or fully appreciated.

But the unfortunate attitude which prevails in the advertising community is one which suggests that there is not much than can be taught the art student except, perhaps, techniques. This conclusion seems logical enough since some designers and art directors whose formal education is limited frequently make brilliant contributions to popular art. Neither their brilliance nor their limitations are proof that a rigorous art education should be denied the majority of art students. Implicit in these feelings is the awareness that you cannot teach art in the same way you teach mathematics or a language. In a beginning class in mathematics the problem is to teach all students to do the same thing; in a beginning art class the problem is to inspire each student to do something different. And there are as many ideas in art as there are in any other subject. Art is not an affair of the heart alone. It is the persistent myth of the noble savage which refuses to see in the creation of a poster a work of intellect. "There are always plenty of honest and energetic people," Joyce Cary delights in telling us, "who regard all systematic education as corruption of the young and innocent, that it belongs to the dark ages of the world when tyrants laid down the law in every department of life. Any such attack on any teaching institution is immensely popular; it promises the student glory without work, it suggests that there is no real difference between the educated and uneducated man. Or, rather that the latter is superior."

Misconceptions about the art director

What is wrong with the education of the art student is the misconception concerning the function of the art director and the importance of his art. For the professional art school to fulfill its moral obligations and for industry to receive artists who are not illiterate in their own language and ignorant of any other — in short, unaware of ideas outside their immediate concern — we need an art education that is both visual (the making of images and ideas through art) and verbal (the understanding and making of images and ideas through words).

Lack of verbal competence — not visual competence — on the part of the art student, the inability to read and to understand and to translate the verbal into the visual and to combine the verbal and the visual meaningfully, produces unimaginative technicians in the profession and visual inanities in the graduate's portfolio. What the art student needs is not so much a change of curriculum as a change of heart; not so much a knowledge of other subjects as a feeling for other subjects; and not so much a knowledge of the arts as an awareness of the interrelationships of the arts.

And those of you who have been fortunate enough to teach at some time in your career know well what Harold Taylor means when he talks about "the enormous resources of talent and idealism in American youth, their lively minds, and their willing hearts." Yet the American student with rare exception, here and there in special schools, has been receiving an inferior art education on the secondary level, despite the dedication of teachers who care.

The claim has been made, and with some justice, that because the curriculum in secondary schools is so heavily weighted on the verbal side, the education of students interested in art suffers thereby and the visual education of those students interested in other fields is practically non-existent. And it is certainly true that the unfortunate practice of using the standard intelligence test as an index of creativity compounds the confusion and adds to the unreliability of predictions about talent. Artists have known this fact for a long time. It is only recently that educators, psychologists and guidance counselors have been willing to admit it. Nevertheless, it is true also that academically talented students with an interest in art are in no appreciable numbers deciding on careers in art. Quite the contrary is usually true. The best academic minds are being won over to other fields. In practice what usually happens is that the academically mediocre who possess some art ability are encouraged to pursue art as a career.

But every parent knows the significance of art in nursery schools, elementary schools, and colleges which train teachers for nursery schools and elementary schools. By the time the student reaches high school, however, art as a required subject has virtually disappeared. And for the student to submit courses in art for college entrance credit is to court disaster. In competition with highly organized subjects like science and mathematics, art finds itself still unorganized and lacking in continuity from grade to grade. A soft spot in the curriculum, it is open to students considered too dull to enter engineering or too disturbed to be tolerated anywhere but in the art department. It takes the art student from three to four years in a professional art school to find out he is not a pariah and to recover from feelings of inferiority. Some students never recover. That he need not always belong to an underprivileged minority comes as a joyous awakening.

The advertising community's responsibility

A fair share of the responsibility for the depressed state of art education must be borne by the advertising community. The image persists of the art director as someone who teeters between martinis and bourbon and branch water, boldly announcing to the world that it is what's up front that counts while proceeding to make posters about it. And it persists with a newer and fancier version which now says that it's what's underneath that counts.

109 About 10 or 15 years ago, it would have been difficult to find many examples of advertising art consistently maintaining the quality offered by Container Corporation. Today, examples of quality abound. And it is heartening indeed to see the importance given to art in the recreation of *McCall's* and *The Saturday Evening Post.* Similarly, the increasing number of creative art directors from print and audio-visual art who have become vice-presidents is a sign of encouragement, and should receive wider dissemination.

In the face of this evidence of the importance of art in advertising, to maintain, as some die-hards do, that the captains of industry have insinuated themselves in a conspiracy to foist bad art on the public is simply ridiculous and ignores the problem. Industry and individual clients choose bad art in the first place because they generally don't know the difference (and are not always shown the difference), and secondly, because bad art is easier to make. It is equally absurd to maintain that the public gets what it wants. Would it not be closer to the truth to say that the public does not know what it wants and is "brainwashed" into accepting what is offered it?

The organization of modern industrial society predisposes men to be mass-minded. Advertising art can intensify this predisposition or choose to lessen it. But the people have very little control over the sound and spectacle that envelop them. Sentimental historians suggest that the masses in other times, when the population was smaller, held independent views about good and bad taste, good and bad art. The masses never revealed more discriminating judgment or taste than they do now. How could they? They were always spoon-fed and under-educated. If the art products that they formerly accepted were less banal, less mediocre than now, that was because such products were never intended for them but for the educated.

"Art for general consumption is always on a lower level than art produced for the educated." But the inevitability of ever-increasing masses of people entering the market as consumers of art produces some incalculable results. Mass-produced art not only ruins people's taste, renders them incapable of thinking for themselves and presses them into conformity, it also engages the interest of the majority for the first time in fields of endeavor that they were totally unaware of before. Thus the way for criticism and opposition is kept open. Hence, to disavow responsibility for public taste is to assume that "the power of discriminating good from bad art and consciously choosing the good [is] something which can safely be left to the 'uncorrupted' spontaneous feelings of the masses." Such an assumption mistakes good taste as the root instead of "the fruit of esthetic culture." (Hauser)

What I have been attempting to suggest should in no way be construed as a plea for a more aristocratic view of art education. It is merely a reaffirmation of what Socrates showed when he characterized the public as the greatest of all sophists. My plea is for a new wave of humanism through art, which will suffuse our culture and help preserve creative individuality before each of us is replaced by the wizardry of electronic computers.

I have no quarrel with technological advancement; it is the world's blessing. It holds forth for all mankind the hope of an abundant life. The machine, however, is an ambivalent creature capable of enslaving and liberating modern man, at once and by turns. The essential values which technology leaves out are the personal values of art. In particular, I am referring to those values which enable the individual to hold out against the force of public sophistry, to engage in work for the joy of working, to find inner peace through individual achievement and to be free, rational and capable of brotherly love.

To some, man's plight seems absurd and the land of humanism has become the wasteland of inhumanity. But we need not succumb to despair. Although wounded, we are not perforce foredoomed. Some people are, some are not. Some of those who are not find zest for living through art as an antidote against apathy and unhappiness which surrounds them. Such a goal as I have been indicating requires more than financial aid, although generous financial support of art education is crucial. The new humanism through art requires recognition of the place of art in the curriculum at the secondary level, in the colleges and universities, in the professional schools and in the lives of all the people. It is not enough for artists and educators to be the guilty conscience of our age. It is for us to bring the sleeping images out of the wasteland into the light.

what to communicate? european graphics: a search for purpose

KEN BAYNES
Assistant Editor,
Graphis, *Zurich, Switzerland*

Let me warn you, this is an artist's view of events. I don't apologize for this but it is as well to say so right at the start. What I am giving you is my own personal view gained from being in the Assistant Editor's chair at *Graphis* in Zurich; but it is me and not the chair talking.

If you caught a visual communicator in a cage what would he look like? A smart agency man? A television director? A wild film-maker scanning Picadilly Circus for raw life? A neat, smart, fashionable free-lance designer with his businessman's patter and knowledge of trends? A fairy-tale maker like Chagall? A city-planner armed with intricate knowledge, trying to make old towns fit modern traffic? A kid scrawling on a wall with tar? A clown falling on his arse? A baby holding out his arms to be picked up? Any of these. Do they have anything in common? They are all makers — makers of ads, of smart offices, of films, of pictures, of cities, of messages, of gestures. All of them want to make something of as high a quality as possible. All are sharing in one facet — the visual — of man's gigantic expenditure of energy in making and communicating. Why are they doing it?

I talked to a man in a pub who said, "Cor. Steaming Hell, you bloody artists are on to a good thing; sitting around on yer bottoms all day with them nudes prancin' all around yer. Cripes!" and he drank his beer quickly, his adam's apple jumping up and down until he leered at me through the bottom of his glass: "Cripes, ho Cripes, what a life," he repeated. Of course, he was right. Artists *are* on to a damned good thing. But not for the reasons he thought. We do these things because we enjoy doing them. In other words we — like everyone — *are* communicators and the visual medium is the one which works for us. Making objects, buildings, stories, films, and so on is what brings us satisfaction and sometimes pleasure — though we may be in Hell if the object in hand does not work properly, does not come out right, gets mangled up by other considerations, is adapted, overlayed, messed up, spoiled. The artist, the architect, the industrial designer and the craftsman are luckier than most because they haven't shared in the alienation from making which is part of the curse of industrial society — a curse which has turned the various kinds of artist into experts on islands instead of spokesmen for a commonly held set of beliefs. But, even for us, the progress from embodying the word of God to being a specialist jam salesman is a sad one. We are like those characters in search of an author; we need a good story to animate us and put blood into our veins, we are searching for a purpose. Of course, this search is not peculiar to Europe; in some ways it appears more strongly felt in America. In Europe we are cushioned around with the ends of the *beaux-arts* tradition. We have an immense variety of people and places from sans-serif, aseptic, neat and tidy Zurich to smelly, rich, comic-drawing Paris; from royal-pompous, old wood-cutty, wide-open, bad-tastey cockney London (a city in a cup of tea) to old, always new, fine-arty, piazzed pedestrianed Venice (a city in a dish of scampi). Perhaps, in this variety, it is more easy to avoid the coldest winds of crude senselessness that come from out-and-out commercialism. But the search is strong here too — and the disillusion is sometimes very deep.

Perhaps for the first time — though there have been periods of great doubt and questioning before — the real problem is not "how" to communicate, though as professionals this must fascinate us most closely, but "what" to communicate. In this we search and do not find.

How can I talk in this way when the books are full of good graphics? The books *are* full, but the streets are *not*. It is easy to show that what good graphics do exist are the result either of special patronage or the result of carrying out certain kinds of work which can, by their nature, avoid the dilemma of communicating intangibles in a society without ideological baggage.

Felix Muckenhirn — (Switzerland)

Functionalism in a technological society

Let us take functionalism first: this is the only completely formulated philosophy of modern design in a technological society that exists. It claims to be an answer that will resolve the dilemma we have been talking about by declaring it irrelevant. It would like to see design accepted by industry as a special kind of science. It bends over backwards to be water-tight and logical — to exclude or limit untidy irrational elements like taste or sexual desire. In fairness to it, it *does* lie behind much of the best work being done in Europe to-day. Allied with a symbolic conception of abstract signs it is becoming an international method. Functionalism represents a good marriage between the logic of a purely scientific approach to design — design by program perhaps — and the art for art's sake of abstract painting. Its great attracting power for designers is due to its showing *some* way ahead. In its framework the artist abidcates much, but at least he has something of his own left; he ceases to be the unemployed romantic and dreamer he thought he might be and armed with polemic, reason if not rhyme, he sets off to be the world's messenger boy, communicating like mad the words and ideas that our society throws around like confetti. And he has become an excellent communicator in such areas as technology, medicine,

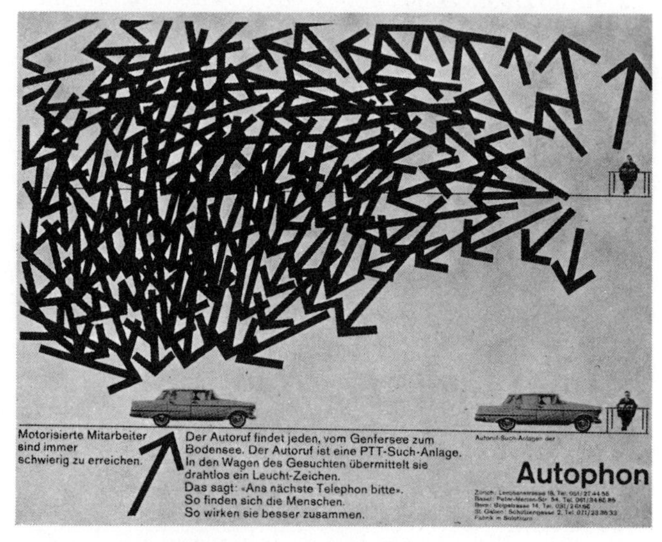

An advertisement by Fred Murer (Zurich) for an automobile telephone

Jorg Hamburger/Pietinen (Zurich)

schedules and all forms of codifications; areas where information is more important than expression. The sans-serif letter has actually become the sign by which we recognize a publication or object designed to give us sober facts of one kind or another.

Sober facts, miles and miles of them, the statistics and numbers, the formulas and relationships that make our complicated old muck-up of a scientific society go jogging along with not much more than a riot or two, a strike or three, a divorce or fifty. Unfortunately, functionalism is *too* persuasive, and as it gets more and more successful it becomes more and more important to find out where its fallacies lie. This is particularly the case when it tries to fulfill needs in which the old dilemmas and problems of art are not irrelevant but of vital importance.

We should realize that the feeling that the communicator can become simply a mouthpiece, as neutral as possible, in the service of his master, is nonsense. The designer who thinks of himself as a hole through which the winds of communication blow is deluding himself. When he takes his nice neutral photograph and his nice neutral type and arranges them in a nice neutral way he is imposing on his message a style as rigid and as recognizable as that used by Leupin. A very particular style results from this so-called neutral approach and it is a style which is too tongue-tied to say certain difficult things well.

Perhaps because functionalism originated in Germany, that country of ruined Romanticism, its rationalism is overly oppressive. It is possible to adopt what is good in it, but when I see the gorgeous world of André François or a Chaplin film I understand at once, with my heart not my head, the weakness of it; the gap in functionalism that must be filled before it can become entirely admirable. There is nowhere to go for a laugh: there is no sentiment and not quite enough love.

Clearly functionalism is something of a special case; but in what other circumstances is good work being done?

Poster by the Polish artist, Jan Lenica, for a production of a Sartre play

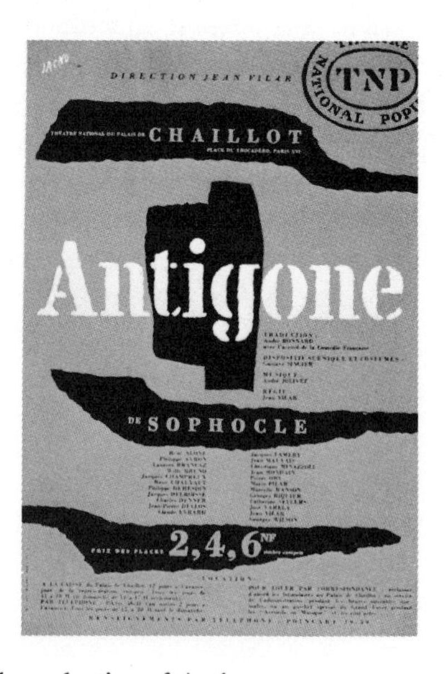

Poster by Marcel Jacno (Paris) for a French production of Antigone

Cultural advertising in Eastern Europe

It is worth taking a close look at graphic art from Eastern Europe for it presents a very interesting parallel with what has happened in the West — though for different reasons. Functionalism has made little progress on the Eastern side of the iron curtain: its rigors do not suit the poetic sensibilities of the Czechoslovakian, Polish or Russian artists any more than socialist realism does. They are expressionists, not abstract designers. There is now much greater freedom in art than there used to be; at least for export. Fine books come from Czechoslovakia. The magazine *Polska* looks like a sophisticated version of *Paris Match* devoted to the latest developments in Polish art and literature. In Poland, Czechoslovakia and Russia, there are fine and lyrical children's books which give new life to the old folk tales. Trnka's puppet films catch perfectly the magic land of the fairy-story. A whole list of things, a rich flowering, but one limited and held to the specifically cultural — held to the fine book, the film poster, the theatre poster, the announcement for an art exhibition. What is astonishing is not that the chink through which this creative energy flows is so narrow but that it is, in many ways, so similar to areas in Western Europe, other than functionalism and corporation patronage, where good and lively graphic design can be found. Posters for art exhibitions, for films, for the theatre, for limited editions of fine books, the list is un-nervingly the same on both sides.

Poster by the Polish artist, Henryk Tomaszewski, for a film festival

Poster by Hans Hillmann (Frankfurt) for a German distributor of foreign films

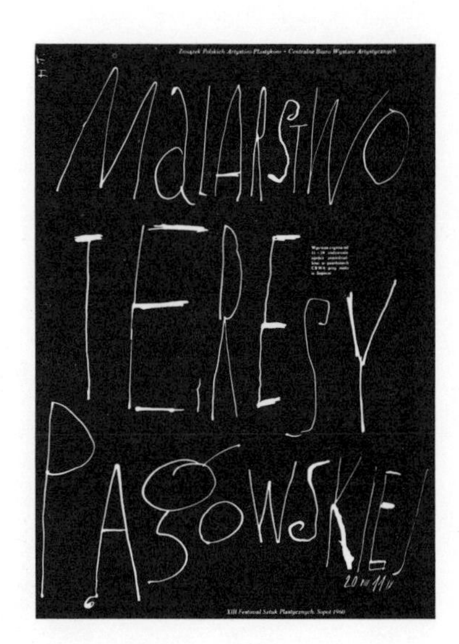

Poster by Henryk Tomaszewski (Warsaw)
for an exhibition of paintings

Poster by Herbert Leupin
(Basel) for a printer

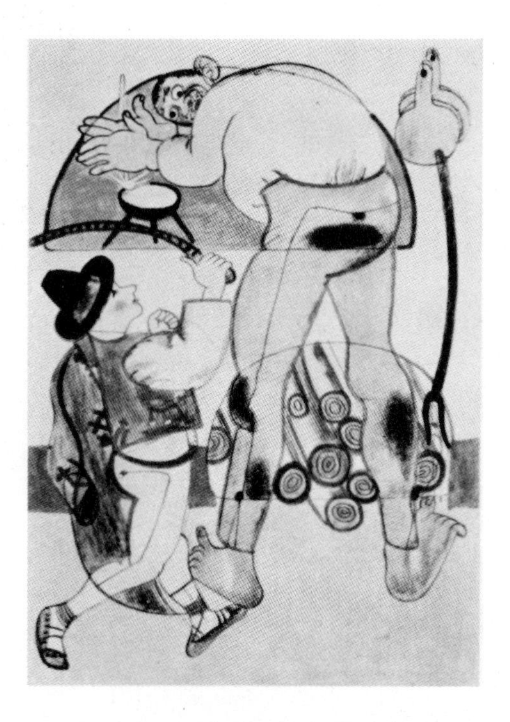

Children's book illustration by Antonin Strnadel (Prague)

Children's book illustrations by the late Hans Fischer (Switzerland)

An Olivetti poster by F. H. K. Henrion (London)

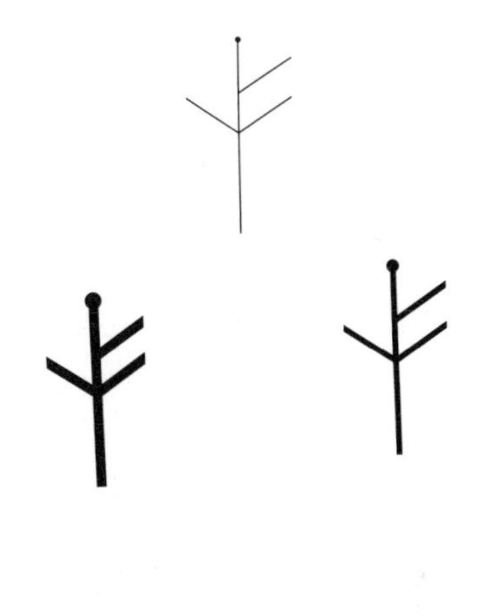

Trade marks by Hans Schleger (London), for Finmar, a Scandinavian shop.

Corporation patronage in the West

If we now add to the Western list the big corporations and firms that have a stake in modern design for one reason or another, we shall have nearly exhausted our sources of good patronage. In the corporations much depends on a single enthusiast — a Pick of London Transport, for example, or an Olivetti. But these big corporations have some advantages in fostering good design; the majority sell an expensive product to an educated public, they are after an image of quality and an image of reliability. They wish to appear as generous patrons so that people will love them. Poor devils, who ever loved such a thing as a corporation? But still, their desire is good for the designer and some of the best graphics in Europe are created from this need. Of course the most classic example of this kind of patroning must be that of Olivetti, who has succeeded in supporting good design in many countries.

Those three — functionalism, specifically cultural advertising and corporation patronage — are the particular cases and the work done around them is rich and exciting, it gives us pleasure and it gives us hope. Sometimes I think it is a danger: the existence of some good patronage, of some good graphics, of people who seek after high standards can act as a sedative to the general ugliness and lack of fine things which surrounds us day in and day out on the way to work and on the way back from it. Just as the existence of Corbusier has not made the average suburb beautiful, the existence of a few artistic posters has not touched the dreary continuity of visual squalor in the run-down east-ends of most European cities. There is some good work but the nub of the problem is left untouched.

Too much "visual squalor"

In fact, good graphic design is desperately rare in Europe just as it is everywhere else. Outside of the specific area of "cultural" advertising and apart from places where one man can make his enthusiasm felt, it presents an equivalent of suburbia. It is an ugly heap of jam salesmanship that sells jam but nothing more.

Mrs. Jones down the road is still hit over the head with a blunt instrument made of corny sentimentalism, childish jingles, cheesecake and smashed sex oozed through a dime novel. It sells, but nobody loves it and why should they; and nobody loves doing it and why should they?

We are so lost today after the great stir-up of values and the explosion that has created a mass society, that we are content with immediate notions that make very little sense even to ourselves. Who would have thought that a situation could occur in which people would feel that it was reasonable and satisfying to make an object *solely* and *specifically* for the sale of jam without any other purpose whatever — no joy, no beauty, no fairy-tale, no laugh, nothing real? And *then* we wonder why we are unhappy!

We cannot take our skill to bits and say something thoroughly banal with enthusiasm. We are betraying ourselves if our posters give nothing other than the urge to buy to those who see them. We *are* good at selling jam; we are *not* good at making a city which communicates meaning and purpose to its inhabitants, and I do not believe that we can take the two things apart. Our own cynicism destroys our audience, and incidentally ourselves.

Advertising is a popular art or it is nothing more than a set of cheap tricks to sell merchandise and if we accept that it is nothing more than a set of cheap tricks to sell merchandise we might as well all pack up this moment and go home. And the people looking at the ads will buy and buy and buy and surround themselves with jam and then go away themselves to plant gardens or build cathedrals out of match-sticks or engrave the Lord's Prayer on a pin-head or shoot themselves because our failure to communicate joy and love and purpose will be a part of a bigger and more colossal failure in which we shall have played our part.

Herbert Leupin (Basel)

Advertising must be a genuine popular art

It would be easy to say that the ordinary man has run out on culture; but I do not believe that. Nor do I really believe that culture has run out on the ordinary man, though I think it has to some extent. It is rather that the ordinary man's cultural heritage has been shoved out of existence by the industrial revolution which mechanised his entertainment. Rubens never was mass-culture, nor was Michelangelo. It is not so much that art has lost an audience but that an audience has lost its art. I fancy that advertising is a popular medium but that it has not become a popular *art* and that there is the rub for us as artists who want to practice it.

For our good and for everyone else's, advertising has to change from being the dull old sledge hammer it is into a genuine popular art. And this cannot be done by a trick, it can only be done truly or not at all.

What is popular art anyway? The most obvious thing about it is that it is popular; that it really means something to the people who see it; that they remember it and talk over it; that it enriches their lives and enlarges their experience. Where advertising most obviously fails is in being un-

Ronald Searle (London)

popular, in leaving people cold. A popular art has its heroes, its exponents who are known by name like pop singers. How many graphic designers are known by name to the people who look at the hoardings? There are some, and their case is a most interesting one for the light it throws both on advertising and on popular art. We can count the graphic artists who people know by name on the fingers of two hands and they are all great humorous draughtsmen: For example, Ronald Searle, Raymond Savignac, Herbert Leupin, André François.

Perhaps a few others. Hearteningly for us they are also artists of great caliber; almost alone they put on the hoardings of our cities first-rate art

Raymond Savignac (Paris)

which is a coherent whole. Theirs is a unity of poetry and life rather than design and it is one which has immediate appeal. In Richard Hoggart's book, *The Uses of Literacy,* which is much concerned with popular culture, I found this which is about the working-class people of the North of England but which has an obvious wider significance. Hoggart writes:

> "Hence the cheerful man, the wit, the 'card,' is still very highly regarded. He makes jokes at work and the time passes twice as quickly; he 'makes y' laugh'; he is 'right funny.' Or he sells you things on the market and you know he is a twister, but still you 'can't 'elp laughin.' He is the big, fat, round-faced, middle-aged man with a pint of ale in the cruder cartoons and picture postcards. He is the real working-class hero, the cheerful, not the romantic, hero. He is a man somewhere

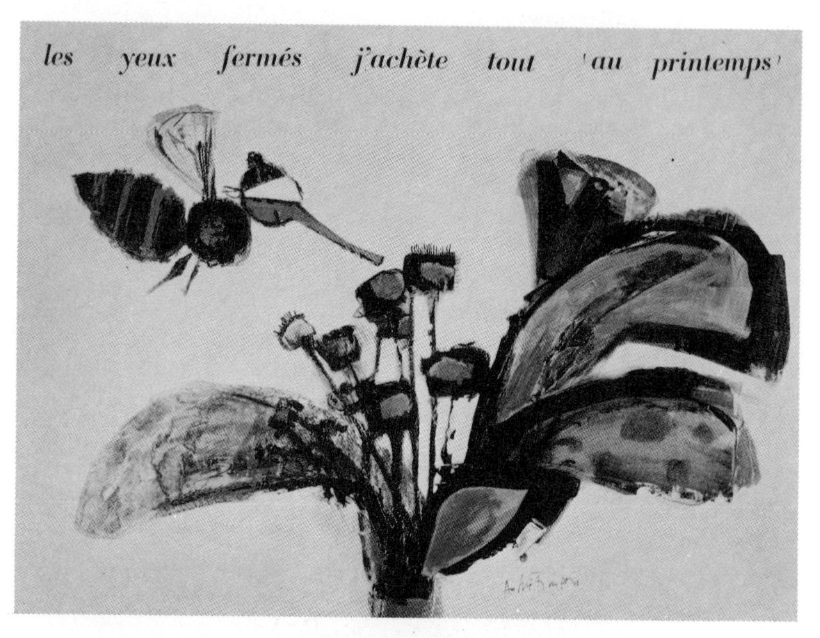

Andre Francois (France)

above forty, who has had a few knocks and knows how to take them, not a handsome young man. The working-classes have always loved a 'comic,' as their biggest music-hall names indicate. They love the men who are 'fair Irish,' full of a cock-eyed fun, and the women who are uninhibitedly and irrepressibly vulgar, like the late Nellie Wallace."

Since most genuine popular visual art has been shoved out of existence by the entertainment industry, we have to try and reconstruct a picture of what a really popular advertising art might consist of from other sources.

It's not so difficult, but it turns our whole business on its head, throws consumer research and all that out of the window, makes us artists again and makes our audience back into people instead of organisms to be bullied and conditioned like Pavlov's dogs. It means good-bye to all the business of hidden persuaders, dressed-up motivations and motor cars that equal married bliss. It means hello to the open persuaders of beauty and excellence, humor and the belly laugh.

Frank Lloyd Wright, at a party in London said: "America can now see the atom. So what? If only she could see William Blake." Perhaps he asked too much, for now it would do if only we could see a plastic daisy without trying to sell it to our neighbors as better than a real rose.

in the beginning, wasn't the picture: mass media communication

GILBERT SELDES
Dean, The Annenberg School of Communications,
University of Pennsylvania

At the outset, I should say that I am not really hostile to the graphic arts but I think, in the back of my mind, that there is some sense to the title of this piece. I think it rises out of my incapacity to understand mathematics and my grave doubts about a certain mathematical formula, namely that "one picture is worth a thousand words." Indeed, I think this old Chinese proverb might have been re-written as, "a thousand pictures are worth one word." If, however, it is true that one picture is worth a thousand words we should, all of us, be dealing with pictographs. Then any concept, any idea that we couldn't express in an image — in a picture — simply wouldn't exist or certainly wouldn't exist in our minds.

Now, I can think of two sentences with about three and a half words in each that I am sure are, as words, worth a great deal more than any picture. I believe that I know a third one, too.

The two I am sure about are these: "I'll kill you." "I love you." These two groups of words are superior, in their effectiveness, to any picture that you can produce. The third sentence I am not so sure about is: "E equals MC square."

But I am not really defending the statement that, "In the beginning was the Word." Quite recently, by accident, I discovered that what is represented by the English word, "word," came from the Greek word, "logos," which was translated, according to my source, as "in the beginning was a plan." Goethe said, "in the beginning was the deed, the act, the fact."

However we take it, I don't think of any of these things as hostile to the original meaning of the word, "image." It is very difficult to use that word now, however, without inverted quotation marks or an apology — although we do make graven images, in appropriate places.

We are all in the business of diffusion, of letting knowledge spread. I have another term for spread, in this connection: letting ideas proliferate. I am in a business which, in a sense, is teaching other people your business. I wish I knew more about your business to teach them.

But let me tell you the unofficial motto of the school of which I am the head. It is this: "If, in the long run, you can't tell everybody what you're doing, what you are doing is worthless." What pleases me about this is that it is not a statement from Madison Avenue. It was made, I believe, at St. Andrews University in Edinburgh — certainly not by an advertiser or a communicator.

Irving Slater said: "If you can't tell everyone in the long run, what you are doing is worthless." I put this up to a distinguished American physicist, who cocked his head and said: "You cannot, in the long run, hope to tell everyone what you are doing." But the hope is good enough. We are in the business of spreading what we know, spreading what we hope we know.

We meet a certain hostility in those people who like to think of themselves as the civilized minority, the happy few. Now, both of these concepts come to us from an aristocratic society, an impoverished society — the happy few, the civilized minority.

Even at the lowest point of our economic cycle, the reverse of what President Roosevelt said was singularly impressive. For the first time in history — he couldn't put it this way — he had an argument to make. But, for the first time in history, two-thirds of the nation were well clothed, well nourished and well housed. This was a fantastic thing because, in past history, only a small minority could really say that they were well in any respect.

As a parallel to this, for the first time in history we have the machinery that can create such a highly civilized majority that one may say a whole nation can be civilized. We have that machinery. We also have machinery to blow ourselves up. But if we avoid the one we can use the other. That's the choice we have to take.

129 I once talked to people in an art museum about doing a television program. I had previously done one with Francis Henry Taylor — the first art program ever presented on television on a consecutive basis — and he had observed that television is for the graphic arts as important, as significant, as the invention of print was for literature. Very little has since occurred to prove what Taylor said, but at least he was willing to make that statement.

When I was talking to these other people, however, they said: "You know, it's no use doing this. People must come into the Museum to see the pictures; there is no way in which you can see certain pictures unless you go and stand in front of them."

Actually, the techniques of reproduction of the arts have been so refined nowadays that it is extremely difficult to tell which is a reproduction and which is the original. Yet, some people say that unless you go in and see the original work of art you cannot claim that you have known anything about it. My opinion is that you can get an enormous amount, a very high degree, of artistic satisfaction out of reproductions. This does not mean that you should avoid museums, of course, but that you should at least get whatever you can.

The feeling behind this hostility to all the mass media is that if "they" — those monsters, the mob — can share it, it can't be very good. There is a feeling that the place in which a thing exists, or the people who present it, determine its value. If the picture is in an art museum, it is art. If it's like "Krazy Kat," in a comic strip, it's vulgar. The fact is that every art museum worth its salt has put away in its cellar about five times as much work as it is showing, and no one wants to look at those works in the cellar. Still people will say, in effect, if it happens on these walls — yes. If you get it elsewhere — no. One must not be too rude about this, however; there are vested interests.

For instance, take someone who has studied music for ten years. He has invested all that time in his studies; then you and he go to a concert. He cannot conceive of your getting as much pleasure from this as he, because you have not put his ten years of work into it. That is *his* vested interest, to keep it away, so to speak — to say that it is special and, in effect, that you're not good enough to enjoy what I enjoy, and I am the superior person.

If I were to suggest that there is a possible lack of confidence in all this, I should be going into analysis, of which I really know nothing. But I always suspect the person who says, "Unless you have made a study, you cannot possibly understand what all these things are really about."

To what degree do you have to corrupt in order to diffuse? How sensational must the "trailer" be in order to make them go to see that movie? I go back to another program, one which I had suggested originally. The idea was to interest people in the arts, not to take the place of an art education but to excite them so that they would want to learn more, to read books, to go to museums. My suggested title was "Scandal in the Arts." For example, consider the "Naked Maja," which was thought to be so scandalous that before they put her picture on a postage stamp they dressed her.

I suggested that there were dozens of these things, not all immoral or sensual but often political scandals — there has always been some scandal connected with works of art. If there were a 30-minute program, three or four minutes could be devoted to a scandalous episode; for the rest of the program contemporaneous works by the same artist would be discussed — in short, a cultural program. But this idea was rejected as being an impropriety. Why? Because you were attracting attention in some way, presumably, that would spoil the capacity of the audience to follow whatever else you were doing. Don't imagine that this is some peculiar thing limited to the arts, however.

When you have the feeling that you are corrupting something, that you are not "putting it over" in its pure state, just figure out the loss. If you do not deliver the thing in its absolute purity as the artist intended, if your loss is under 10 per cent and you gain 1,000 times over in diffusion, if 1,000 times as many people get 90 per cent of the subject, then I think that it is really worth doing. You will re-attract part of this vast audience — to go back to the original, to hear it again, to read a book and so on. You cannot then say, "Unless we give it to you precisely as it was intended, we don't give it to you at all." For one thing, there are many arts in which you just cannot do so.

Most of the old masterpieces are dulled by time, and they're not at all what the old masters intended. For example, we haven't any idea what Beethoven really meant in the structure of anything he wrote for the orchestra because we do not now get the sound of the instruments he was writing for. There are 50 ways of producing "Hamlet" or "Macbeth." Those who say the one thing that cannot be done is to produce either properly on television are completely crazy, because there is no standard of the "proper" work. If several millions of people a year would see a good production of "Hamlet" or "Macbeth," and if the price you had to pay for this was reducing the text, the printed text of the original, to precisely the same character that the printed text of a Beethoven symphony is now, I would say that this was a good price.

131 We are a little inhibited about the printed text of any great work, but what is really happening to us now is that we are in the middle of a revolution. This is a basic sort of revolution, the best example of which was the introduction of print itself. The economist, Harold Innes, had a theory that any time there is a revolution people communicate with one another. What we are now in might be called, in fact, a counter-revolution. We are coming out of the era of print into that of electronics, and this is largely an era concerned with the projection of images.

Robert: What I'd say is that we don't "communicate." quote, unquote! We try to pursue a Reality as we see it — & if our pursuit is honest enough & lyric enough then other humans can understand what

2. we have perceived. Matisse at Vence is a marvellous example of this.

At the dedication ceremonies for the Chapel he wrote "As you all know

3. I have NOT pursued Beauty (beauté) but Truth (la Verité) & he went on to say that he'd spent his whole life trying to set down the TRUTH.

If we work this way on a book or an ad

we don't "communicate"

ROBERT OSBORN
Author and Illustrator

What I'd say is that we don't "communicate," (quote, unquote!) We try to pursue a *reality* as we see it — and if our pursuit is honest enough and lyric enough, *then* other humans can understand what we have perceived. Matisse at Vence is a marvellous example of this. At the dedication ceremonies for the chapel he wrote: "As you all know I have *not* pursued beauty but truth," and he went on to say that he'd spent his whole life trying to set down the truth.

If we work *this* way on a book or an ad or a speech, there will be conviction and therefore it will be convincing. We won't take any polls, no tests will be run, no women's pulses held. We won't attempt to *guess* what people want, what people are like, what degree of cuteness or smugness or snob appeal will be cranked into our message. Instead, we will try in all honesty to pursue how things look to our eyes, our feelings (to Emerson's, to Picasso's, to Roger de la Frenaye's, to Chagall's and, above all, to Leonardo's). If we get it down at all the way they did we'll begin to communicate all right! Have no fear!

And we'll speak surely and clearly to other humans just the way the simplest Rembrandt drawing speaks, or Piero della Francesca's "Resurrection" grabs you by the throat and holds you planted in that Tuscan room.

The instincts have been brought to bear — not just tricky, calculating, chilly intellect, but *all* of a man, and his heart excited and beating.

There is no point in saying it again — all of those adults ought to know this simple fact by now. But somehow they deceive themselves that there is another way around, that somehow one can speak to other men and women without reality in your voice or in your eyes. I've never seen it work that way, but they think it can. Look through *Life* magazine to see what a farce advertising makes of reality or of genuine human feelings and needs. Boy! Look at the world pictures and then see the ads next to them. It's liver-shaking!

I repeat that the point of all of this is that those ad-drawers and copy-writers ought to know this by now — and telling it to them isn't going to help. They profess that they want to straighten up and really communicate but they go right on cranking out the same diluted, color-added, frill-laden *imitation* of reality which doesn't shout or scream but only gives a giggly whisper of what *anything* is about.

Next year, why don't they announce in advance that they wish to gather and earnestly discuss our *money*-oriented culture. If they talked honestly about it they would understand why they *now* "communicate" as though they had a cold potato in the right side of their mouths.

Officers of the Art Directors Club of New York 1961-1962

Edward B. Graham: *President*

Bert W. Littmann: *First Vice-President*

A. Russell Hillier: *Second Vice-President*

John A. Skidmore: *Secretary*

Mahlon A. Cline: *Treasurer*

Wallace F. Hainline

Mitch Havemeyer

John Jamison

Franc Ritter

Otto Storch

Edward R. Wade

Marie Archer: *Executive Secretary*

Conference Committee

Robert O. Bach: *Conference Director*

Arthur Hawkins: *Conference Chairman*

John A. Skidmore: *Executive Board Member*

Hoyt Howard: *Operations*

Edward P. Diehl: *Photography*

Joan Levine: *Conference Secretary*

Edward S. Morse: *Publicity*

Donald Kubly, James Miho, Henry Guarini: *Conference Designers*

index